## Praying for Godly Character

"Are you ready for a real adventure? Ignite your prayer life with this 40-Day guide and see what God will do!"

| Award-winning author Amy Robnik Joob

## Praying a Blessing for Someone

Why waste your time worrying for a loved one, when you could spend that same time praying powerful prayers of salvation, breakthrough, and blessings instead? Join Eric Sprinkle and Laura Shaffer as they give you the blueprint for prayers that make a world of difference.

| Linda Evans Shepherd, bestselling author of Praying God's
| Promises and Praying Through Every Emotion

## Praying for Someone's Salvation

Thoroughly comprehensive, practical, clear, inspiring and helpful. HIGHLY recommend.
    Laura Shaffer along with Eric Sprinkle, has used her gentle, comprehensive and long-ranging experience of intercessory prayer to compose a guiding book which is user-friendly, encouraging and hope-inspiring. Hang on in there. Keep praying.

| Early Amazon Reviewer

I like this book because the prayers are sooo much more powerful and give me ideas on what words to use through the day. See, I'm 8 1/2 and my friends at school do not know Jesus. This helps me focus.

| Amazon Reviewer (with Mom)

I've been doing the 40 Day Prayer Guides—Praying for Someone's Salvation for about 2 weeks now and it's such a huge blessing. The prayers are wonderful, and working through each day's prayers has definitely been a blessing to me each morning. I am actively seeking time with the person I am praying for as a result of praying for him and we have had a lot of fun... plus it has laid a groundwork of trust for God to work in through our conversations.

> Robin Shear, professional Joy Coach, author of the JOY BITES blog & an upcoming book about finding joy despite difficult circumstances. (www.joytotheworldcoaching.com)

---

## Praise for the 40 Day Prayer Guide series

You two make such a great team. Not only is Laura's content rich and practical, but Eric's photos also add a powerful and needed dimension to the prayers. Well done!

> Dick Bruso, Branding/Marketing Expert and Founder of "Heard Above The Noise"

You can pick up this book and begin praying immediately because the prayers are right there for you. Laura guides us as a "prayer warrior," sharing her words and letting us make them our own. Thanks to this book, applying prayer is easier than ever before."

> Laine Lawson Craft, best-selling author of *Enjoy Today Own Tomorrow*

I love the images and photos in these books. They are such an inspiration! Some of them excite me, others spark my imagination. And sometimes, one of them will completely transport me away to another place. A beautiful, quiet place, far away from life's stresses, where I can sit for a minute, reflecting on God's goodness, and on my wonderful prayer time with Him.

> Susan Neal, RN, MBA, MHA Director, Christian Indie Publishers Association, and best-selling author of *7 Steps to Get Off Sugar and Carbohydrates*

I loved this guide to pray blessings over others. Working through it not only blessed those I prayed over but also ended up blessing myself as well. Many of those I prayed for also ordered the book and began praying blessings for those in their lives. What an impactful way to change the world (or at least the lives of our friends and families) through prayer.

> Kim Clinkenbeard, certified fitness coach for women over 40 and best-selling author of *Fitness. Food. Faith: Your Eternal "Why" for Everlasting Results* (www.getfitwithkimtoday.com)

## 40 DAY PRAYER GUIDES

# Praying for Your Pastor

Powerful day-by-day Prayers Inviting God
to Bless and Direct their Lives

## Eric Sprinkle and Laura Shaffer

*"Fanning the flame within"*

*Praying for Your Pastor, Powerful day-by-day Prayers Inviting God to Bless and Direct their Lives*

Copyright @ 2022 Eric Sprinkle and Laura Shaffer

All rights reserved. No part of this publication may be reproduced or transmitted in any form or by any electronic or mechanical means including photo copying, recording, or any information storage and retrieval system now known or to be invented, without permission in writing from the publisher or the author.

Scriptures taken from the Holy Bible, New International Version®, NIV®. Copyright © 1973, 1978, 1984, 2011 by Biblica, Inc.™ Used by permission of Zondervan. All rights reserved worldwide. www.zondervan.com The "NIV" and "New International Version" are trademarks registered in the United States Patent and Trademark Office by Biblica, Inc.™

All photos by Eric Sprinkle
Cover and interior design by Robin Black

ISBN: 978-1-7322694-6-0

Published by Adventure Experience Press in partnership with the fine folks at EA Books Books Publishing, a division of
Living Parables of Central Florida, Inc. a 501c3

AdventureExperience.net
EABooksPublishing.com

# DEDICATIONS

**Laura**
To the Pastors of churches I've attended since I was a baby,
and to the Military Chaplains who served in our Armed Forces here and abroad
who I heard preach most of my life, and to the Sunday School, Vacation Bible
School and Worship/Choir teachers God has placed
in my life throughout the years—
some I heard speak many times, some became close friends.
I thank you for the dedication to the Calling God placed
in your heart and on your lives.
I thank you for the words you spoke, the messages you delivered,
for the prayers you prayed, and for the living examples you were that became
guidance, direction and an education for me and others.
I thank you for taking on the mantle that put a huge target
on your back from the evil one.
May you and your families all be blessed for generations
with God's continued best protection for fulfilling
His purposes in and through your lives.

**Eric**
For all the Pastors I've had the privilege to sit under and learn from. From
Noah and Jimmy to Matt and Josh and every small-town preacher and Military
Chaplain in between. Thanks for everything gents, you simply can't imagine
the impact you're all having this side of eternity.

# ACKNOWLEDGMENTS

- The Team at EABooks for once again helping us create, format, and put this book together.
- Editor Amy, for taking a break from the falling Carolina leaves to look over this for us.
- Huge thanks to Pastor Josh in Montana and all the Beta Readers for all your useful thoughts and ideas.
- So many thanks again to my amazing prayer partners over the years who have been a blessing in my life, teaching me how to pray by example through our Torah Group, Moms in Prayer groups, our Church Small Groups and Bible studies. Their prayers and encouragement are invaluable.
- Extra thanks to my current Pastors Kyle, Peter, Scott, and Stephen who gave me insight into things they would want and need prayer for. And my friend Laura on our church staff.
- Eric also wants to thank Panera Bread in Colorado Springs, Denton, Texas, and Bossier City, Louisiana for a place to lay his laptop while doing final edits.
- Last and always, to our Gracious Lord God, who not only hears our prayers and gives us Pastors to 'feed us with knowledge and understanding', but also blesses us far beyond what we could ever dare to ask or even hope to imagine.

*Soli Deo Gloria* indeed.

## INTRODUCTION TO THE 40 DAY GUIDES

Okay, who wants a really big target on their back? Wants God to hold them to a higher standard than others? Raise your hand. Anyone?

Take another look at the front cover of this book really quick. This is what it looks like when a large group of water molecules all get together, powered by the warmth of the sun.

So what happens when a group of Believers all get together, empowered by the Holy Spirit to pray for their Pastor?

Now there's a good chance you're already praying for your church leadership - during busy holiday services, and Vision weekends, but what if we changed that up a bit? What if we prayed for them, intentionally, for the next 40 days?

Let's face it, our gracious Lord God has a thing for 40 days. Forty days of rain to flood the earth, 40 days before the clock ran down on Nineveh to return to Him, 40 days spent in the wilderness before Jesus started his ministry. Over and over, we see 40 days as the time frame God uses for major changes in people and circumstances.

So as you pray for your Pastor, how about adding in their spouse, their kids, and their own work/life balance too. Asking God to inspire them with a vision for your church. Fanning the flames for the lost in your own community, and around the world. In a world where Pastors get taken out by adultery, drug use, and simple burn-out each and every day, what would happen if you stepped in and asked God to especially protect them? Strengthen them to stand against all the temptations and distractions.

Would your church flourish more? The people, the kids, the volunteers? Would you?

God loves it when we talk to and share with Him through prayer. Share our thoughts, our fears, our celebrations, and concerns. The Bible tells us it's our prayers and petitions, with thanksgiving, that God uses to bring us peace (Phillipians 4:6-7). Jesus himself told the disciples that sometimes when casting out demons only prayer will do the trick (Mark 9:29).

Maybe it's just me, but I get the feeling that I've vastly underestimated just how powerful prayer can be—and maybe you've felt that way too.

Let's make beautiful, Bible-based, laser-focused prayers a part of our daily routine for the next 40 days. Prayers for either one-Pastor-at-a-time, or the entire staff all at once. And instead of trying to think of the words, we'll use some wonderful, powerful, stirring prayers from your new friend Laura.

Let's read her prayers and make them our own. Let's pray them silently or aloud, inserting the name(s) of your Pastor along the way. Don't worry, it'll be almost automatic by the time you get to Day 4.

What if we add a second one to pray for? Or invited someone else to pray with us too? What if your entire men's or women's group went on this 40 day journey together? The entire congregation even? Or just you and your spouse, every morning over coffee, lifting up your church leadership, asking together for our gracious Lord God to impact their lives and ministry. To reveal Himself. To align them to Him. To bless them with safety and clear direction in their leadership with Our Lord God.

Our Heavenly Father loves hearing our requests to Him through prayer. He loves blessing us with gifts too, often far more than we could ever ask or imagine.

So what does He want to do in the lives of your church Pastor? And maybe your church congregation as well?

I say we find out.

It's time to turn the page and begin a 40 day journey, focused on praying blessing over those who've been called to lead your church. One that's going to impact them, and you as well.

Are you ready?

Let's do this.

---

*Thinking of walking through this book with a church group or as a body? Sounds awesome! Connect with us at 40DayPrayerGuides.com for some amazing bulk discounts for anyone ordering more than 10 books. This is going to be great!*

# Introduction to Praying for Your Pastor

Pastors and ministry leaders often have a spiritual target on their backs. Meaning that the evil one, the devil, really has it out for them. If they could get a pastor to somehow fail personally—morally or financially, or relationally with their family or congregation, or at the business of running a church, then many people might lose confidence and possibly turn away from their faith. Or perhaps not a total failing, but just being distracting or overwhelmed at work, with problems in their marriage or with their kids. Even the stresses we all have to live with every day can build up and become defeating. And anything that would diminish their impact is a 'win' for the other side.

And very often the people pastors serve don't have a good idea of how to pray for them. We don't understand the challenges they face on a personal level: with their families, relationships, time, and influences—social or spiritual. Leaders are held to a higher standard than you or I. Church leaders, to an even higher degree. And they need our help.

> Exodus 17:10-13, *So Joshua fought the Amalekites as Moses had ordered, and Moses, Aaron and Hur went to the top of the hill. As long as Moses held up his hands, the Israelites were winning, but whenever he lowered his hands, the Amalekites were winning. When Moses' hands grew tired, they took a stone and put it under him and he sat on it. Aaron and Hur held his hands up—one on one side, one on the other—so that his hands remained steady till sunset. So Joshua overcame the Amalekite army with the sword.*

Aaron and Hur supported Moses when he needed it. And now—here's your chance.

Like Aaron and Hur, we can be there to prayerfully support our pastors. And not just when they are tired or stressed. Anytime God puts them on our hearts.

To gain insight into what would be beneficial, we gathered suggestions from pastors and ministry leaders as to what they would ask people to pray for them. And with the mindful purpose of helping people pray intentionally and consistently for them, we created 40 prayers to uplift, encourage, support and protect our pastors.

# FOREWARD

After overcoming an early addiction to alcohol, God called my husband Clint to pastoral ministry.

Flash forward to later in life, with over ten years of successful ministry behind us, when God called him to ministry in a rural community, over two hours from friends, family and his semi-pro football team. Balancing family, life-giving ministry and self-care presented a challenge, but somehow Clint made it work.

During this time, a retired clergy member took Clint under his wing. They visited shut-ins together, talked over ideas, and commiserated on the struggles of ministry with each other. One bitter January day, Clint's mentor slipped on icy stairs, hit his head, and fell into a coma, dying just a week later.

Clint performed the funeral.

Seven months later, Clint's pain became unbearable. He purchased alcohol at a gas station, drank it, and got behind the wheel.

He woke up the next morning in the hospital.

Ephesians 6 says our battle is against dark, spiritual forces. When men and women put their mouths to microphones and speak the gospel to masses, they place spiritual targets on their backs. Clint was no different. Displaying grace and understanding beyond our comprehension, the church re-instated him. At this same time, another truly remarkable thing happened, too. Clint's colleagues called him and shared their struggles too.

"We're talking about divorce."

"I have a porn addiction," another said.

"I'm an alcoholic, too, but no one knows."

My husband passed away only two years later, but until that time he pastored other pastors who possessed very few safe spaces to share their dark secrets.

Your pastors battle real flesh and blood struggles, just like you. Unlike you, they aren't free to share those struggles because pastors are expected to skirt a line close to perfection.

In my experience, every pastor I know struggles with -
Loneliness
Spiritual Warfare
Discouragement
Sin and compounded guilt for sinning.

After the accident and later, Clint's death, there existed about a three-year span of time, during which people would ask me, "How are you still standing?"

"On the prayers of my friends," became my reply.

Your prayers make such a difference and are truly felt by those you pray for. I commend you and thank you so much for holding up your pastor in prayer.

**Samantha Evans**

> Author of *Adventure Devos* and *Love Letters to Miscarriage Moms* and an upcoming book: *The Rocky Path of Mourning*. "Mrs. Evans, Reverend Evans has been in a car accident... and we found something on the CAT scan." Find more at LoveSamEvans.com.

# How to Use this 40 Day Prayer Guide

## Prayer Pages:

The guide will give you one daily theme with requests to pray for your pastor for 40 days. If something interrupts your schedule, pick up the next prayer when you can.

You can simply pray the prayer to yourself or out loud as it is, or you can let the Holy Spirit guide you and use your own words.

Or these prayers can be a springboard for your prayer time as the Holy Spirit brings more things to mind as you pray.

For instance, there may be times when a particular problem or situation will take precedence over a pre-planned agenda of prayer.

And there may be times when the Holy Spirit leads you to a different topic for blessing or need. Go for it.

It is our hope to help you be more intentional and consistent in praying. And by spending time in prayer, you will grow more familiar with and open to the Spirit's leading. Being flexible and sensitive to the Holy Spirit is the most important thing.

## Reflection Pages:

Every seven days the Guide will give you opportunities to:
- Write down your thoughts as you go along.
- Evaluate your progress.
- Look for ways God may be answering your prayers and thank Him.
- See how He is speaking to you personally about your prayer life, or how God might be leading you in your life.
- Consider ways you might connect with your pastor.

## Appendix Pages:

Check out our Appendix at the back of this book for valuable resources you might need during your 40 Day Journey or after.

Whether it's how to put on spiritual armor before praying, praying Scripture prayer for your pastor, or how to know if you're hearing God, we've got you covered.

# Before Beginning

We hope to encourage you and accompany you on your 40-day journey with day-by-day prayers. We also understand that sometimes things get in the way that are unavoidable. If you have to miss a day, simply pick up where you left off. You don't want to miss out on the blessing of a prayer or of hearing from God.

It may help to find a specific place or regular time of day to be sure you are being intentional and consistent in your praying (like when you first get up, or while exercising, on your way to work or during a break from work, or in a place in your home at a certain time, or at a natural break in your daily routine).

When praying for another person, often called intercession, or interceding, there is wisdom in preparing yourself as well. Two areas are important:

1. **Confession and Repentance**—The Bible tells us in Psalm 66:18, "If I had cherished sin in my heart, the Lord would not have listened." So it is important to take time to ask God to search your heart and show you any sin you need to confess and repent of before you move into interceding for someone.

   God has promised that "If we confess our sins, He is faithful and just and will forgive us our sins and purify us from all unrighteousness" (1 John 1:9).

2. **Spiritual Armor for Battle**—Paul tells us to be "Strong in the Lord and in His mighty power. Put on the full armor of God" (Ephesians 6:10-11). So we need to do that—name and pray on each piece before we pray for others.

Appendix A and B at the back of this book will walk you through these steps.

# Prayer Tips

Are all prayers equal? It seems that God has listed some guidelines for us in Scripture that can either compromise or boost the effectiveness of our prayers.

There are even things that can cause Him to choose to step back or even disregard our prayers for a time. Yikes! Others are just the opposite, creating a multiplying effect on our prayers.

Have a look through and make sure nothing listed is going to get in your way over the next 40 days.

## Some Biblical Guidelines

- *The prayer of a righteous person is powerful and effective* (James 5:16).
  Be sure you're following God and steering away from anything unrighteous or purposefully against God's ways for living. Holding grudges, being angry, indulging in wrongful thoughts or actions can all take away from the effectiveness of your 40-day journey.
- *The eyes of the Lord are on the righteous, and his ears are attentive to their cry* (Psalm 34:15).
  Exactly the opposite, we can rest assured we have God's complete attention when pursuing right living in our actions and choices.
- *Then Jesus told his disciples a parable to show them that they should always pray and not give up* (Luke 18:1).
  No worries there, you're going to be praying for the next 40 days, so you've got this!
- *When you ask you do not receive, because you ask with wrong motives, that you may spend what you get on your pleasures* (James 4:3).
  Okay, so praying for your pastor to be blessed just so you get to be a giraffe at VBS this year is not allowed, agreed?
- *But your iniquities have separated you from your God; your sins have hidden his face from you, so that he will not hear* (Isaiah 59:2).
  Again, let's be careful we don't have sin in our hearts that will get in the way of what we're asking. If we want to see the stars, let's get away from light pollution. If we want to talk to God, let's clear out the background noise and use a strong signal with four bars.
- *This is the confidence we have in approaching God: that if we ask anything according to his will, he hears us* (1 John 5:14).

Let's all be sure we're asking for things in line with His will, His plans, His timing, and not our own. Trust that God is actively working to guide and direct your pastor and bless them for His Glory, even if we're not seeing anything happening right away.

## Additional ideas that can boost the impact of your praying

- Pray these prayers out loud.
    *Does it help God hear them better? No. Does it help you? You bet! Praying out loud helps you slow down and focus on the person and words you're praying—allowing time for the Holy Spirit to meet you in your prayer. And that can make a difference all on its own.*
- As the Holy Spirit brings additional things to mind when you're praying, pray those too.
    *The Holy Spirit knows best what this person needs and what will bless them.*
- Pray the daily prayer multiple times a day.
    *When you eat. Morning and Evening. Or maybe when you start your car. Whenever you think of the person you're praying for.*
- Pray for more than one person
    *What happens if you say two pastor's names for each prayer?*
    *Or pray for the group of pastors in your church*
    *Or for the pastors of your faith as a group*
    *Or pray for the pastors of different faiths in your community as a group*
    *Or pray for all the military chaplains. See a special Prayer for Military Chaplains in Appendix C*
- Pray this 40-day journey with a friend, or group.
    *Together, lift up the same pastor in prayer.*
    *Or each of you pray for your own pastor if you attend different churches but check in with each other on your journeys.*
    *Or get a Women's, Men's or Youth Group to pray for your pastor.*
    *Or have your Bible study group pray for your pastor.*
    *Or a pray for a group of Deacons, Elders or Staff.*
    *What would happen if every member of the congregation was invited to take this 40 Day Journey with you? At the very same time? Asking for Blessings together? Petitioning for safety and wisdom for your pastor together?*
- Consider fasting at some point during the journey.
    *Giving up TV, social media, or even certain foods for a week during your journey will only serve to sharpen your spiritual focus!*

There are, of course, many things you can pray asking God to strengthen, protect, guide, and bless your pastor. This is not meant to speak to all of them.

It will, however, help you be more intentional and consistent in praying. And by spending time in prayer, you will be open to the Spirit's leading. Learning to listen to the Holy Spirit guide you is most important.

It is our desire to help you grow in your prayer life as you pray for others. And that those you pray for will benefit from the answers to your prayers.

And that you will be blessed as you Lean in and Learn from the Lord through prayer.

# Table of Contents

| | | |
|---|---|---|
| **Day 1** | My Commitment | 3 |
| **Day 2** | Health | 5 |
| **Day 3** | Spiritual Protection | 6 |
| **Day 4** | Marriage | 8 |
| **Day 5** | Children | 10 |
| **Day 6** | Family | 12 |
| **Day 7** | Heal Broken Places | 15 |
| **Day 8** | Praying Scripture—Matthew 6:9-13 | 19 |
| **Day 9** | Identity and Calling | 21 |
| **Day 10** | Make their Life a Stage | 23 |
| **Day 11** | Time Management | 25 |
| **Day 12** | Pray for their Spouse | 27 |
| **Day 13** | Free from Anxiety | 29 |
| **Day 14** | Joy and Humor | 31 |
| **Day 15** | Praying Scripture—Psalm 23:1-6 | 35 |
| **Day 16** | Good Shepherd | 37 |
| **Day 17** | Messages | 38 |
| **Day 18** | Bring People | 41 |
| **Day 19** | Hearing God | 43 |
| **Day 20** | Lifelong Mentoring | 45 |
| **Day 21** | Wisdom | 47 |
| **Day 22** | Praying Scripture—Ephesians 3:14-21 | 53 |
| **Day 23** | Time with You | 55 |
| **Day 24** | Solution to a Problem | 57 |
| **Day 25** | Committed Friends | 59 |
| **Day 26** | Courage | 61 |

| | | |
|---|---|---|
| **Day 27** | Vision | 62 |
| **Day 28** | Divine Appointments | 65 |
| **Day 29** | Praying Scripture—Psalm 20:1-9 | 69 |
| **Day 30** | Spiritual Power | 71 |
| **Day 31** | Unity of Staff | 73 |
| **Day 32** | Encouragement | 75 |
| **Day 33** | Coping with Trials | 77 |
| **Day 34** | Property | 79 |
| **Day 35** | Building | 81 |
| **Day 36** | Praying Scripture—Psalm 27:1-3, 5-8, 11-14 | 85 |
| **Day 37** | Congregation | 86 |
| **Day 38** | Confidence | 89 |
| **Day 39** | Teachable | 91 |
| **Day 40** | Aaronic Blessing | 93 |

| | | |
|---|---|---|
| **Afterwards** | Thank You After 40 Days | 99 |
| **Appendix A** | Confession and Repentance | 101 |
| **Appendix B** | Spiritual Armor for Battle | 102 |
| **Appendix C** | Prayer for Military Chaplains | 105 |
| **Appendix D** | Week of Prayers for Spiritual Power and Protection | 106 |
| **Appendix E** | How to Tune in to God's Voice | 114 |
| **Appendix F** | Tune in Exercise for Hearing God | 116 |
| **Appendix G** | Hearing from God | 118 |
| **Appendix H** | Hearing God Worksheet | 120 |
| **Appendix I** | More Info on Images | 121 |
| **About the Authors** | | 123 |
| **Appendix J** | Additional Resources | 124 |

# ANOTHER BATTLE

You call me to the battle once again
enemies abound on every side
I look to see what weapons will avail
the one that speaks the loudest is: Abide!

I place Your armor on it is the best
protecting head to toe and side to side
I take my shield and sword and make my stance
And still the Spirit speaks to me: Abide

My marching orders come and in I go
once again into the battle's fray
I have no fear of losing for I know
that at the Finish You will win the day

I do not fight alone You send me help
other Mighty Warriors by my side
It's hand-to-hand and swords are clashing now
and still I hear the word from You: Abide

We make a strong assault and push them back
it seems the enemy faints and runs to hide
and in this show of strength our Battle Cry
continues to encourage us: Abide!

The enemy was only gathering strength
and makes a mighty push that sends us back
Some are wounded and they step away
others stagger hurt in the attack

The battle isn't over, night has come
We pitch our tents and dress our wounds inside
The wind keeps blowing fiercely through the dark
But peace commands our spirits to Abide

We will be strong to fight another day
and into Heaven's Victory we'll ride
our Battle Cry will strengthen all the way
For in our Mighty Savior we Abide

**Laura Shaffer © 2-24-2020**

# DAY 1

## My Commitment

Ephesians 3:14, 16-17, *For this reason I kneel before the Father... I pray that out of his glorious riches he may strengthen you with power through his Spirit in your inner being, so that Christ may dwell in your hearts through faith.*

In the Power of the Name of the Lord Jesus Christ, I am offering these prayers for You to act and effect Your will during these 40 days of prayer for Pastor _____. Draw them into a closer relationship with You by pouring out blessing on them that they will recognize has come from You.

Heavenly Father, I cannot even imagine all the forces currently influencing Pastor _____'s life. And Pastor _____ is just as human as the rest of us. These forces temp us, divert us, and overwhelm us. The world misleads, our flesh distracts, and the evil one lies with the intent to destroy.

The devil is against You and all that is holy, seeking to harm, kill and destroy our lives. So much more the life of someone who has dedicated their life to the calling to lead a church, preach the gospel, and encourage believers. Evil forces in the spiritual realm seek to keep people away from You and trapped in darkness. They seek to distract and discourage, defeat and depress pastors. They attack Pastor _____ personally in areas of faith, health, strength, marriage, family, and professionally in the church. Sowing distrust and disunity they stir up confusion and bring calamity. They keep pastors from seeing how You work and bless their lives. And not only Pastor _____, but also attack their kids and spouse.

I will pray these 40 days for Your protection over their body, mind and spirit. Watch over Pastor _____'s physical health so no illness sidelines them. Meet their emotional needs where relationships have been broken by betrayal, unmet expectations or dishonesty. Heal any spiritual wounds where Pastor _____ has been hurt, misled, or believed lies. Be their Healer: Jehovah Rapha.

I will put on Your spiritual armor every day for these 40 days (Ephesians 6:10-17). And I will stand in the gap for Pastor _____. I will intercede for them, asking You to give them victory over the enemies of their soul.

I humbly ask for Your will to be done in and through Pastor _____'s life. Father, open up the storehouse of blessing, and let Your love and blessing pour over them and meet their needs. Let this remind them that You have called them, You are with them, and You greatly care for them always. Amen

# DAY 2

# Health

3 John 1:2, *Dear friend, I pray that you may enjoy good health and that all may go well with you, even as your soul is getting along well.*

Heavenly Father, I acknowledge that Pastor _____'s life is Yours. As You hold it so carefully in Your hands, provide good health and healing to Pastor _____. Help their body work as You created it to work. Protect them from illnesses and accidents. Strengthen their immune system to avoid simple or serious diseases. Help their bones, muscles, mind, heart, and other organs grow and stay strong.

As Pastor _____ matures and ages, provide the physical, mental, sensory and relational stimulation, motivation, and encouragement they need for a healthy lifestyle. Whether on the golf course, pickleball court, or shooting hoops with friends or kids, help them stay active. Help my pastor's mind stay sharp, and their hearing and sight be excellent to take in all the things of Your amazing world. Keep their mind, eyes and ears turned away from evil, lust, pornography, and focused on good, wholesome and godly things.

Where there is physical illness or injury, be their Jehovah Rapha, their Healer. If Pastor _____ is unaware of a weakness, or disease, bring it to their attention in the earliest stages and lead them to the right doctors, treatments, medications, or therapies that will work in concert with Your healing power. Do not let my pastor ignore symptoms that are telling them any part of their body needs attention.

Bring Pastor _____ the discernment to know if treatment is needed, and the courage to move forward. Send medical teams who will be fully focused, using all their skill, knowledge, experience and expertise to treat my pastor.

Help Pastor _____ be mindful caring for their body. When tired, give them sweet and regenerative sleep. When hungry lead them to make wise choices, not allowing stress to drive them to eat foods that offer convenience without solid nutritional value.

If there are habits my pastor needs to change with diet, exercise, or weight, then lead them to make changes in those areas providing the encouragement and strength they need to follow through.

Thank You that You have created Pastor _____'s body in such a miraculous way, with redundancies and healing abilities within itself. Speak health into their bones, organs, their whole body, blessing them with good health. Amen

# DAY 3

# Spiritual Protection

Ephesians 6:12, *For our struggle is not against flesh and blood, but against the rulers, against the authorities, against the powers of this dark world and against the spiritual forces of evil in the heavenly realms.*

Heavenly Father protect and guide Pastor \_\_\_\_ in their comings and goings. You tell us that *our enemy the devil prowls around like a roaring lion looking for someone to devour* (1 Peter 5:8). And delights in getting anyone to sin or doubt their faith. How much bigger is the target on my pastor's back!

There are spiritual enemies who seek to undermine Pastor \_\_\_\_'s faith and ability to do the work You created and called them to do. So I pray *against the rulers, against the authorities, and against the spiritual powers of this dark world, and the spiritual forces in the heavenly realms* who set themselves up against You and Your will for Pastor \_\_\_\_, to protect their life, health, family, relationships, home, school or work, finances, mental and emotional well-being and spiritual growth.

Thank You for the armor You give Christians to wear when doing battle with these spiritual enemies. Call Pastor \_\_\_\_ to put on the Helmet of Salvation which guides and guards their head: thoughts, attitudes, dreams, visions and revelations, what they hear, see, smell, taste and speak.

Father, help my pastor focus on things that are good and pure and godly. Keep them clear of fear, doubts, insecurity, or feelings of unworthiness. When negative thoughts come, remind Pastor \_\_\_\_ that their identity comes from the truth of who You say they are: a child of God, chosen, holy and dearly loved (Colossians 3:12).

Remind Pastor \_\_\_\_ to put on the Breastplate of Righteousness. This protects their body and heart, and stops fiery darts and deflects blows from the evil one. No personal or professional attack of harsh words or attitudes will defeat my pastor.

Call my pastor to tie the Belt of Truth around their waist to discern truth from lies; so as not to be misled by deception, misinformation, or dishonest speech. Father, in their personal relationships, business or church dealings, help Pastor \_\_\_\_ recognize truth, and walk in it.

Remind Pastor \_\_\_\_ to place the Shoes of the Gospel of Peace on their feet, saying they are ready to accept Your marching orders at any time. Guide them, and shine a light on that next step so they can see and overcome obstacles in their path. Give them peace in a world where people are frustrated, wanting to vent their anger. Let peace fill Pastor \_\_\_\_'s heart when encountering angry people. Strengthen my pastor with energy for the journey You have them on. And help them leave behind goodness and mercy in their path.

Keep Pastor \_\_\_\_ protected this way in Your awesome spiritual armor. Amen

# DAY 4

## Marriage

Ecclesiastes 9:9, *Enjoy life with your wife whom you love...*
*(If your pastor is not married, replace this prayer with one from Appendix D)*

Heavenly Father, bless Pastor \_\_\_\_\_ with a person who will love You, and love them. Knit them together as one, to love each other and to serve You with their marriage. It's a tall order to share a mate with Your call on their life. Grant them both the ability to understand what is required of a ministry marriage. And give them a supernatural ability to withstand that challenging but blessing-filled relationship.

Where money is concerned, help Pastor \_\_\_\_\_ and their spouse accept what comes from You with gratitude. Let them have open, honest discussions about their financial needs and long-term goals. Even in difficult times, help them seek You in setting priorities.

When communicating, let Pastor \_\_\_\_\_ and their spouse speak the truth in love, with words that encourage and build up the other. Help them be good, patient listeners to the other's point of view. When arguments do occur, I pray for respect and forgiveness to preside, without bad language or harsh tones.

With church responsibilities, help them set appropriate boundaries where each actively supports the other's calling, trusting You to guide ministry decisions; and each works to ensure the other is a high priority.

Father give Pastor \_\_\_\_ and their spouse a healthy work/life balance with times for rest and relaxation. Adequate sleep is a necessity to refuel energy and attitude. So bless them with sweet, recuperative, healing sleep that allows them to wake feeling refreshed mentally and physically.

Help Pastor \_\_\_\_ and their spouse plan their schedules for relaxing together, finding activities for recreating together - with and without children present. In that enjoyment, let it build closeness and energize their relationship.

In addition, help them make time for intimacy a priority: uninterrupted times with the energy and right attitude to meet each other's needs physically, emotionally, sexually, and spiritually. Encourage them both to communicate honestly about their personal needs. And keep their desire alive throughout their marriage to please each other with adequate time to provide for physical, emotional, sexual, and spiritual intimacy.

Keep Pastor \_\_\_\_'s love life pure for their mate. When meeting with members of the opposite sex, provide adequate visibility from others even in business or counseling situations. Let it be a protective rule to allow a third party to be present to keep all activity and conversation appropriate and above board. When traveling, protect my pastor from the temptation of inappropriate meetings or pornography. Let the remembrance that they are Yours be a powerful deterrent and an awesome reassurance. And that You are available anytime, for company and the courage to resist temptation.

Give Pastor \_\_\_\_ and their spouse the ability to show each other their love in ways that the other will appreciate. Lead them to understand the other's love language, and find ways to give each other outward, encouraging expressions of the love and commitment they have for each other.

Let their love be sweet and all You intend it to be for married couples, regardless of the cultural and society values of the times. Let Pastor \_\_\_\_'s marriage be sexually fulfilling, and the emotional, spiritual and physical bonds strong enough to withstand extramarital sexual temptation.

Strengthen Pastor \_\_\_\_'s marriage in all stages of life, in good times and in difficult ones. Let the couple come together to rejoice, celebrate, solve problems, meet challenges, endure hardships, and comfort each other in sorrow. Truly enjoying their life and love. Amen

DAY 5

# Children

Psalm 127:3, 5, *Children are a heritage from the Lord...blessed is the man whose quiver is full of them.*
*(If your pastor has no children, replace this prayer with one from Appendix D)*

Heavenly Father bless Pastor \_\_\_\_\_'s children, and send Your ministering angels to guard and zealously protect them. Keep these children healthy and free from life-changing accidents and illnesses. Watch over their comings and their goings so they are safe, from the time they are infants, through the childhood and teen years, all the way to adulthood.

Give my pastor's children energy and mental clarity to grow and learn what they need to in order to become physically, mentally, emotionally, socially, and spiritually mature. Let their creativity and spontaneity spark fun and joy as they play and grow. Help them share their toys, emotions, concerns, trials, and victories with their siblings and parents.

As they eat, learn, play, do chores and care for each other and for their room and pets, help them accept both privileges and responsibilities. Even with the added pressure in being PKs (Preacher's Kids) give them the freedom to have fun and the room they need to make mistakes like other kids.

Teach them to respect their elders and others in authority. Provide godly role models and mentors for them at every age, as coaches and teachers at school, in the home, or at church. Guide their TV watching, books, games; direct and bless all their educational and learning activities. If there are difficulties or challenges, bring those who can identify the best way for these children to learn so they don't get behind in their studies.

Let them make a connection between nature around them, and You, the One who created it all. Teach them to respect life and learn from what You've created. We can learn about life even from watching ants (Proverbs 6:6)! Give these children time to simply observe Your creation and the ability to learn from it.

At every age, keep them close to You, and bring friends alongside who will be a godly influence to help them develop socially and emotionally. Protect them from any who would take advantage of them or lead them away from You by activities, ideas, or language. Even seemingly innocent things can be dangerous spiritually, so give these children supernatural discernment, and the ability to say no.

These children are spiritual targets as well. So protect them from the enemy's attack in all ways. Call them into a saving relationship with You at an early age. Give them an advanced ability to understand spiritual matters, know right from wrong, and recognize temptation.

Protect these children from any who would mistreat them; whether a family member, friend or stranger. Empower them to speak out and get the help they need. Let them sense Your presence, guiding and protecting them, knowing they can call on You and speak to their parents at any time, with any need.

Keep communication open and honest between parent and child at every age. Let them feel love from their parents, and from their heavenly Father; even when they have failed or are in trouble. And show Pastor _____ how to make time for each child individually, teaching them how specially and wonderfully they have been created and gifted by You, their Heavenly Father.

At bedtime, help them slow down, being open to Your quiet presence as they lay down to sleep. Let their sleep be sweet, healing, and regenerative for their bodies, their minds, and their spirits.

Let Pastor _____'s children grow in wisdom and stature and in favor with God and man. Amen

DAY 6

# Family

2 Corinthians 13:11, *Strive for full restoration, encourage one another, be of one mind, live in peace. And the God of love and peace will be with you.*

**H**eavenly Father, help Pastor \_\_\_\_\_ relate well to their immediate family: parents, brothers and sisters, grandparents, aunts and uncles, spouse, children, grandchildren, whatever family You have chosen to bless them with. Whether they live nearby or far away, whether they see each other every day or only on special occasions, bless each one.

Father, protect them from tragedy and trauma. Draw each one of them to know You as Savior, to worship You as a family, and to turn to You with problems. Teach them to seek Your wisdom in making plans and living their lives.

Especially those who live with Pastor \_\_\_\_\_, but also those far away, encourage open and honest communication. Let each family member be able to be honest about their physical, emotional and spiritual needs. Meet whatever needs my pastor has in dealing with the others. Encourage them all to speak the truth in love (Ephesians 4:15).

Father help Pastor \_\_\_\_\_'s family members understand the responsibilities of the leadership position my pastor has. Show the family the real love my pastor has for each of them, but also Pastor \_\_\_\_\_'s love and dedication to the ministry and church You have called them to. Help the family accept the effect it has on their life and the time it requires.

Let my pastor's parents and siblings take on more responsibilities for family care when necessary. Let the kids not fight, and be willing to share Mom or Dad. Let their spouse be willing to find that balance needed to feed their marriage and personal needs while supporting their spouse's ministry call.

When difficulties arise give special wisdom to Pastor \_\_\_\_\_ when dealing with any family members. As they age, challenges can present concerning marriage, jobs, relocations, finances, aging parents, growing children…all the same things all of us deal with in our daily lives.

With relationships, provide bridge-building opportunities for the members to work things out bringing restoration and unity. Help them not fight but get along, modelling love. If there are difficult decisions that bring stress, give Pastor \_\_\_\_\_ Your greater perspective. Open their eyes to a totally unique answer that comes from You. And give them the courage to move forward with that solution.

Father, be with Pastor \_\_\_\_\_ in the hard times that may come. When one person needs grace, let another one in the family have grace to spare. When necessary, let apologies be made, forgiveness asked for, and offered freely. Help the whole family work for restoration of positive, healthy relationships. Let my pastor's family be a source of joy and strength and support for them. Amen

# DAY 7

## Heal Broken Places

Jeremiah 30:71, *"But I will restore you to health and heal your wounds." Declares the Lord.*

Heavenly Father, move into any places Pastor _____ has brokenness. If there have been uncaring people or unhappy circumstances in their past churches, heal those wounds so they can fulfill Your purpose for them in our church.

Where there is hurt, my pastor may have lost strength physically, mentally, emotionally, or spiritually. Wherever there is brokenness, speak Your life and healing. Give Pastor _____ faith to trust what You say: that You love them and that Your love is greater than whatever difficulty they've been through.

Heal those places where Christians have disappointed Pastor _____, let them down, criticized or even caused them pain. Let them separate the pain of being hurt by fallible humans and things that happened in churches, from their feelings and understanding of who You are and all that You have for their future.

Broken places can also create vulnerability to sin or believe a lie. While You are healing them, strengthen and encourage Pastor _____. Send angels to guard them and create a hedge in front and behind, along their sides, above and below them so that no evil power can get in and lead them farther away from You. Encourage them by bringing someone alongside to be wise counsel by checking their attitudes and guiding them in godly decisions.

Father, be their strength and spread Your protection over Pastor _____'s body, mind and spirit. Meet their emotional needs where relationships have been broken by betrayal, unmet expectations or dishonesty. Heal any spiritual wounds where they have been believing lies about themselves or You.

Free them from any past pain, guilt, or shame, to be all You want them to be here, now. Thank You for being their Healer: Jehovah Rapha. Amen

## Reflections

How are you doing so far? If you have been able to be consistent in praying this week—good for you!
If not, what has gotten in your way? How can you remedy that?

_____

If you have missed any prayers, just pick up tomorrow where you left off.

During your prayer time this week, has God shown you anything about Himself? About yourself? About your pastor?

_____

_____

If you know any specific needs your pastor or their family has, take a moment and pray for those now. If you know of any concerns they have with their health, challenges they face with their job, neighborhood, or community, note them here and pray now or include it in next week's prayer time.

_____

_____

_____

If you know the names of their spouse, children, parents or other family members, list them here. When you know of any who are having a difficult time or facing challenges, pray for them by name.

_____

_____

_____

In thinking back over the prayers prayed this week...
If you can see, or if your pastor has mentioned feeling under spiritual attack, or if there is something big happening in your church, consider adding the extra week of Spiritual Power and Protection prayers found in Appendix D. Or pray one of those prayers now.

→ As an encouragement, drop your pastor an email, card or text letting them know you're praying for them. You might ask if there is something specific they would like you to pray?
If they make a request, list it here to include in your prayer time.

_____

→ If you have specific health, marriage or family issues, pray for yourself. Ask God to bring healing to your body, mind and spirit. And bring peace and reconciliation to your marriage and family relationships. Consider writing out a prayer here.

_____

_____

→ If you have felt under spiritual attack, ask God to reveal it. Consider beginning each day praying for forgiveness and putting on the Spiritual Armor God has given you. You can find that information in Appendix A and B

_____

_____

→ If there are past hurts that you still have strong feelings about, ask God to heal those broken places in your spirit. Pray Day 7 for yourself.

# DAY 8
## Matthew 6:9-13

Matthew 6:9, *Our Father in heaven, hallowed be your name.*

Heavenly Father, help Pastor _____ respect and honor Your name. The devil trembles at Your name. And it causes him frustration and pain to hear Your children speaking and honoring Your name.

Give Pastor _____ a desire to see Your will done in their life, and in our church. Show Pastor _____ if there are things they can do here, to help *Your kingdom come and Your will to be done here on earth as it is in heaven*. Then empower them to accomplish those things.

*Give* Pastor _____ their *daily needs*. They need physical protection for their family, and spiritual protection from the plans and efforts of the evil one who seeks to harm, kill and destroy the lives and unity of their family. Meet their family's basic needs of safety, a home, food, clothes, transportation, and the finances and wisdom to keep all those things running.

Make Pastor _____ aware of any sin in their life. Help them take time to come before You, and examine their life in thought, attitudes, relationships, rebellion, and behaviors done, or not done.

Invite them to be quick to *ask for forgiveness* and grant the strength to turn away from that sin. And if necessary, to make any apology or amends to others. Thank You that You are faithful and just to forgive, and will purify from all unrighteousness, removing all my Pastor's guilt and shame (1 John 1:9).

If Pastor _____ needs to *forgive others, lead them* to a place where they are able *to do that*, whatever it may look like. Remind them that no matter the hurt or pain that has been caused, vengeance is Yours. And that they can trust leaving it in Your hands. Even if it takes a long time to completely forgive, put my pastor on that road, empowering them to take whatever steps You direct them to take.

*Do not lead* Pastor _____ *into temptation* or let them be lured into evil by temporary pleasures. Help them see the hook beneath the lure that would draw them into sin. Remind them that temptation will take them farther than they ever mean to go, and will cost them more than they ever want to pay.

But thwart any plans the evil one has for Pastor _____. Let no weapon formed against my pastor prosper. In *delivering them from evil*, let them sense You watching over them and remember that they are Yours. Let that be an awesome reassurance. Amen

# DAY 9

## Identity/Calling

Ephesians 2:10, *For we are God's handiwork, created in Christ Jesus to do good works, which God prepared in advance for us to do.*

Heavenly Father, give Pastor _____ an awareness and appreciation of the unique way You created them. Help them see through Your eyes, who they really are; and let that be the source of their sense of value and worth. You created them; with specific gifts, talents, and personality in preparation for the work You prepared for them. Give my pastor a sense of that work and how those gifts will benefit them in it.

Teach Pastor _____ that their actions do not determine their identity, but that the identity You give them as a child of God determines their actions. As a pastor, an individual, a family member. So whether they're playing with the kids, working in the kitchen, or leading a Bible study, let them find satisfaction in who they are.

Do not allow Pastor _____ to define their worth by the standards of the world. Show my pastor they are more than their job, their salary, or the role they play in relationships. Jobs and relationships carry responsibilities and expectations. And too often our sense of worth suffers if we don't meet someone else's expected level of performance. You love Pastor _____ because of who they are: Your beloved child. And that identity is the greatest value!

Reassure my pastor that You have already equipped them with resources, abilities, and everything they need to accomplish the work You have prepared in advance for them. Help Pastor _____ understand how to use those to accomplish Your will through Your calling on their life. And how using those gifts and talents will bring a sense of accomplishment, satisfaction and joy.

Open Pastor _____'s eyes and heart to opportunities You are inviting them into. Open doors that will benefit and lead them where You are working, and close doors that will not. Don't let my pastor be led astray by the world or anyone else who would seek to manipulate or control them in these choices.

Father, Lead Pastor _____ in the way that is best for them and will bring honor and glory to You. Whatever that looks like for them or our church, shed enough light for them to see and take the next step. Speak in their ear and say "This is the way, walk in it" (Isaiah 20:31). Amen

# DAY 10

## Make their life a stage

Genesis 39:2-3, *The Lord was with Joseph...and his master saw that the Lord was with him.*

Heavenly Father, Pastor _____ lives much of their life in the public eye. In life, they encounter the same problems and challenges anyone else does. Flat tires, leaky pipes, money, pressures at home and work have an impact just like they do on everyone else. Even good things can cause stress: birthdays, vacations, holidays—Christmas.

So many people are watching what they do, looking to them; not only to lead the church, but be an exemplary parent, spouse, neighbor, friend. I pray You would make Pastor _____'s life a stage upon which You act out Your purpose and Your will. So when people look at them, they see You.

Father, be with Pastor _____ as You were with Joseph. Let Your presence enable them to see through any distraction, or deception that might cause them to be vulnerable to temptation. Help them bear up under whatever circumstances might draw them into worry, anxiety, or stress. And let them speak of their faith in You and in Your power to help in hardship and in good times.

Others saw that You were with Joseph, so let others see that you are with Pastor _____ as well; blessing, encouraging them, and working in their life. Show people, through my pastor's life, that You are a wonder-working God! And how much You care for Your people, and desire to have a personal relationship with them.

Pastors are human, and so will err. But let people see that Pastor _____ lives their life for You, and are a godly example to follow—looking to You for guidance—depending on You for insight and understanding—Finding courage to be obedient when You call them to action.

Let my pastor set an example by looking to You for comfort and hope when times are sad or challenging. And most of all, when they have been mistreated, cheated, or taken advantage of, let Pastor _____ walk in the freedom of forgiveness—forgiving those who wronged them, and trusting in You for vindication and vengeance.

Let Pastor _____'s faith be evident to all. Amen

# DAY 11

## Time Management

Psalm 90:12, *Teach us to number our days, that we may gain a heart of wisdom.*

Heavenly Father, don't let Pastor _____ fall victim to the "tyranny of the urgent." Teach them to recognize what things are important from Your perspective, and make time for those. Don't let them get so carried away with what seems urgent that the important things slip by. But give them wisdom in setting priorities and structuring their days. And if unexpected, truly urgent things come up, keep those important things fresh in their mind to get back to.

Father, multiply Pastor _____'s time. Help them work smarter, not harder. Let them see when tasks can be combined to save energy and time. Show them how to accomplish tasks quickly and efficiently. And give them discernment to know when an interruption is just a distraction, and when it is a "Divine Appointment" from You.

Help Pastor _____ see where balance is needed in their life. Multiply their energy and strength to do what is needed on a daily basis. And remind them that rest is important too. Since they "work" on what most people consider the Sabbath, help them set good boundaries for down time.

Don't let Pastor _____ believe the lie that they "work better under pressure" and put off things till the last minute. Or feel like they have to do everything themselves. Show them how to lead from their strengths, and delegate or arrange for others to meet remaining needs.

One of the devil's strategies is to invite us to do things that consume our enthusiasm, time, and energy so we don't get around to doing what You have called us to do. And a pastor has so many responsibilities: preaching, counseling, leading a church, budgeting, staffing, overseeing building maintenance, on top of all their personal relationships. No one can do it all.

And trying to, by burning the candle at both ends, only leads to burnout. That will not bring the godly results You intend for my pastor. Not in their life or Your church.

Father, teach Pastor _____ to live each day to the fullest. Show them how to measure out their time and energy for what is important. Be their guide in setting the flow of their days. Amen

# DAY 12

## Pray for Spouse

Heavenly Father, bless Pastor \_\_\_\_\_'s spouse \_\_\_\_\_ to be the *two* who help each other work or when one falls down. Help them be the other's best friend as they share their lives with each other, and with the church.

Let this spouse \_\_\_\_\_'s life also be full of purpose and joy. Give them a sense of Your presence and peace even in the midst of need or waiting. Draw this spouse into a close relationship with You.

Father bring people for my pastor's spouse \_\_\_\_\_ to spend time with whose company they enjoy-trustworthy friends who will be like iron sharpening iron (Proverbs 27:17). And a mentor to guide them in emotional and spiritual growth and keep them accountable to live their faith. Introduce them to someone they can confide in and who will keep their confidences.

Even with close same sex friends, give my pastor's spouse \_\_\_\_\_ discernment when sharing personal or intimate information that might allow for the temptation to gossip about the pastor. Protect the marriage relationship by limiting opposite sex relationships appropriately so no strong emotional or intimate ties are formed that might tempt them into sexual sin.

Let time between my pastor and their spouse be a priority so they can dream and plan together and meet each other's needs. With decisions, teach them how to work together as a team.

Ensure there is adequate support in each of their lives for handling stress: challenges and problems that arise with family, parenting, school, transportation, home or work. When trials come, help them find answers together, or perhaps with a trusted Christian counselor. Strengthen them to persevere, proving and purifying their faith.

Father, provide for Pastor \_\_\_\_\_' spouse \_\_\_\_\_ to have continued spiritual growth and a deepening relationship with Jesus Christ. Give them a hunger and thirst for scripture and for gaining wisdom and understanding from it that will help guide their life. Provide for fellowship with other believers and give my pastor's spouse \_\_\_\_\_ a place to serve and use the spiritual gifts You've given them.

Grant my pastor's spouse \_\_\_\_\_ such joy in their life that it would overflow and be a light to those around them. Amen

# DAY 13

## Free from Anxiety

Philippians 4:4-7, *Rejoice in the Lord always. I will say it again: Rejoice! Let your gentleness be evident to all. The Lord is near. Do not be anxious about anything, but in every situation, by prayer and petition, with thanksgiving, present your requests to God. And the peace of God, which transcends all understanding, will guard your hearts and your minds in Christ Jesus.*

Heavenly Father, give Pastor \_\_\_\_ a sense of Your presence in rejoicing and in trials. You tell us to rejoice in all things, and yet there are many things that bring feelings of tension, worry and anxiety. You have a Word for that as well. *Do not be anxious…*

This scripture tells what to do—*Rejoice!* Because *the Lord is near.* Help Pastor \_\_\_\_ sense Your presence with them in real and tangible ways so they know they are not alone. Let them turn to You first in those times of worry or anxiousness. Give them signs that You are there and are working with them, protecting them, loving them even through difficult circumstances.

Next, whether in their personal life, or regarding situations in the church, remind Pastor \_\_\_\_ to bring every issue or concern to You in prayer. Let any worry my pastor has, trigger a specific prayer for Your perspective, Your perfect solution, that will bring resolution.

Next Father, provide the help Pastor \_\_\_\_ needs as they wait on You for the answer to their prayer. Encourage them to express thanks in advance that You will provide what they need, and take the burden off their shoulders.

And Father, give Pastor \_\_\_\_ Your *peace.* Your *peace transcends all understanding, and will guard and protect* my pastor's *heart and mind.* Isaiah 26:3 tells us You will keep those who focus on You in perfect peace. In Hebrew, those words are "shalom, shalom" a peace upon peace.

Send Pastor \_\_\_\_ peace like that. So if circumstances cause their sense of peace to wane, send another wave of Your peace, like endless wave upon wave.

Whether finances, relationships, family responsibilities, dealing with people or issues in the church, Father, give Pastor \_\_\_\_ freedom from anxiety. Amen

# DAY 14

# Joy and Humor

Proverbs 17:22, *A cheerful heart is good medicine, but a crushed spirit dries up the bones.*

Heavenly Father, help Pastor _____ find joy and humor in their everyday life. Proverbs tells us that laughter is good medicine for the soul. And a happy heart makes a cheerful countenance (Proverbs 15:13). Bring Pastor _____ laughter and something to lighten his heart every day.

When things are going well, remind Pastor _____ to smile and spread cheer to others. You tell us to rejoice always! So let them find joy in both the expected and the unexpected. Show my pastor it's Your favor resting on them, not luck or fate or some other power in the universe. But that their joy comes straight from You: the Lover of their Soul, the Lifter of their head, the Creator of their very being.

Don't allow the stress of any challenge to overtake Pastor _____'s focus or cloud their mind. When needed, whether it's just been a long hard day or something difficult or troubling has just happened, remind them to take a "Laugh Break!" It could be tickle fights with the kids, watching a funny movie, or spending some time with people who make them laugh. Show my pastor how to release tension, whether it's for an afternoon, an hour, or just cracking a joke or two.

Father, let a good sense of humor lift Pastor _____'s spirit and lighten their burden. Even in times of challenge or trouble, help them be able to laugh and smile. Rekindle their sense of humor and wonder at the world. Let laughter be a balm for their soul, a light in the darkness.

You know Pastor _____ best: the desires of their heart and the depths of their soul. Bless them with a gift that will fill their soul with deep joy, a sense of sincere and honest satisfaction that brings a smile to their face and peace to their heart.

You can give joy in the midst of suffering and pain. You can fill the heart that was weeping, with rejoicing. You are capable of wonders beyond human imagination. You can do miracles!

Job 8:21 says *He will once again fill your mouth with laughter and your lips with shouts of joy.* Let the joy You bring be a source of strength for Pastor _____. Amen

*What did the man say when all his lamps were stolen? I'm delighted!*

# Reflections

Week 2! How does it feel to be consistent and intentional in prayer?
Is it hard? Is it getting easier?
Keep at it—2 weeks! Good for you!
If anything has gotten in your way, how can you remedy that?


If you have missed any prayers, just pick up tomorrow from where you left off.


During your prayer time this week, has God shown you anything about Himself? About yourself? About your pastor?

_____
_____
_____
_____
_____
_____
_____

If you know any specific needs your pastor or their family has, or if God brings something else to mind, make a note of it here and pray for it now or include it in next week's prayer time.

In thinking back over the prayers prayed this week...

→ Consider writing a short note or card or send an email or text to let your pastor know you've been praying for them. If there's a scripture you prayed that you feel your pastor would benefit from, include that. List any scriptures you feel apply.

_____

_____

→ Since your pastor's life is a stage, consider mentioning in the card or in person, something that you've observed in their life where you can see God at work. List some of those things you've observed.

_____

_____

→ Consider writing or telling them a funny story or joke to brighten their day.

→ If any of these prayers has been something you would benefit from, go back and put your own name in the spaces and pray them for yourself or your family.

→ Consider writing your own prayer, or starting a journal of thoughts as you pray. Or write those thoughts here.

_____

_____

_____

_____

_____

# DAY 15

## Psalm 23:1-6

Psalm 23:1, *The Lord is my Shepherd...*

Heavenly Father, *You are the Good Shepherd.* And Pastor _____ is Your sheep. Attend to their personal needs as a good shepherd would so they *lack nothing.* Meet my pastor's every need, even those they may not be aware of.

Remind Pastor _____ to take time to rest and *lie down in the green pastures* You have prepared for them: places that offers safety, nourishment and peace. Do not let my pastor get in over their head, or be swept away by challenging or emotional circumstances. But *lead them* into *quiet waters* where they can *be refreshed.* When Pastor _____ becomes world-weary or feels discouraged, depressed, and are down-cast, renew them. Give them hope, and *bring restoration* to their life, *their soul.*

If Pastor _____ becomes ensnared in the thorny briars of this world, or has wandered away, *guide them* with Your staff *along the right path.* If they find themselves entangled in circumstances or relationships and feel like there's no way out, show them You can make a way. Father, protect them from the traps and temptations of the evil one *to preserve Your name because they are Yours.*

Father, You have walked this earth and are aware of every trial and temptation my pastor will face. Even when Pastor _____ is *walking through the darkest valley*, let them *sense Your presence with them* in real and tangible ways. *Comfort* and protect them by using *Your rod and staff* to direct them, and defend them from any earthly or spiritual predators.

Lend Pastor _____ Your courage to face whatever is before them, even *in the presence of their enemy. Anoint their head with oil,* consecrating and healing them. And *overflow* their life with Your strength, blessing and abundance.

Bring *goodness and mercy* into Pastor _____'s life, so much so that they *leave it behind them* as they interact with people. For their whole life, let them be a source of blessing, forgiveness, encouragement, inspiration and peace.

And let my pastor rest in the knowledge that they will *live in Your house*, be with You, as Your beloved sheep, *forever.* Amen

# DAY 16

# A Good Shepherd

Jeremiah 3:16, *Then I will give you shepherds after my own heart, who will lead you with knowledge and understanding.*

Heavenly Father, thank You that Your eyes are on my shepherd. Empower Pastor \_\_\_\_\_ to be a good shepherd where You have called them. Like a good shepherd, help my pastor seek after You to lead our congregation. And help our congregation follow the pastor, without whom, we would be scattered and vulnerable to the philosophies of men and the ways of the world.

Let my pastor be a leader after Your own heart. Ignite their passion for Your truth and for sharing it with others. Give Pastor \_\_\_\_\_ the messages we need to hear, preaching the whole Word, regardless of social attitudes. Strengthen them to share what we need to hear even if it seems unpopular.

Give Pastor \_\_\_\_\_ a knowledge and understanding of Your Word You have impressed upon their heart. Not just head, but heart knowledge that flows from the Holy Spirit as my pastor is in touch with You. Let their understanding be evident in their example: overcoming temptation, repenting of sin that might give the devil a foothold, and trusting You for direction in their personal and ministry lives.

Father, provide my pastor with a knowledge and understanding of how to reach people. With a passion for reaching the lost, allow Pastor \_\_\_\_\_ the flexibility to be gentle with unbelievers, not expecting them to act or see things from a Biblical perspective. Bless Pastor \_\_\_\_\_ with stimulating, challenging sermons, but never care more about the sermon than the people.

Speak through Pastor \_\_\_\_\_ with great passion and in plain enough language so everyone can understand spiritual truth that will allow and encourage real spiritual growth and transformation in people's lives. Help our pastor educate and equip the church to recognize the schemes of the evil one. And teach us to pray and arm ourselves with Your armor to overcome those schemes and escape the traps set for us.

By watching Pastor \_\_\_\_\_ act justly, love mercy and walk humbly with You, we will learn to seek after Your own heart too (Micah 6:8). And being taught and led with knowledge and understanding, we will be cared for by a good shepherd. Amen

# DAY 17
# Messages

**2 Timothy 4:1-2,** *I give you this charge: Preach the word; be prepared in season and out of season; correct, rebuke and encourage—with great patience and careful instruction.*

Heavenly Father, protect Pastor \_\_\_\_\_ physically, mentally, and spiritually as they prepare messages to share with our church. Gift them with an ability to put together clear-minded presentations of the Gospel in language anyone can understand.

Give Pastor \_\_\_\_\_ fun and interesting stories and life experiences they can use to illustrate and teach powerful lessons from scripture. Don't let them be afraid to share when they made a mistake, laugh at themselves, or even ask for help. Let these illustrations connect with our own everyday life in ways that make scripture applicable to how we should live. And memorable so the lessons will be remembered.

Guide Pastor \_\_\_\_\_ to speak messages of truth into the lives of those at risk because they don't even see the deceptions used to keep people away from the salvation You offer. Or the schemes that keep believers from living the abundant life You came to give. Rather than condemnation, help my pastor confront sin in a way that draws people to a true repentance and willingness to turn away from sin and ask Your forgiveness.

Pour Your Holy Spirit over Pastor \_\_\_\_\_ to bring deliverance to those who are being oppressed or possessed by the enemy. Remove the blinders from listeners' eyes to see the effect the evil one is having and has had over their life, their choices and their spirit.

Make Pastor \_\_\_\_\_ bold in sharing the impact You've had on their own life: how You have answered prayers, delivered them from dangerous circumstances, directed their decisions, healed when sick or wounded, and comforted in hardship.

Strengthen my pastor to talk about how You have encouraged them in their faith over and over again. Let them speak words of reassurance and inspiration to help others who need encouragement.

Father, as a church, we need empowering messages on everything—to: teach us how to live, apply scripture to our lives, reveal the workings of the evil one in the world and our lives, convict and correct our behavior or the way we think, encourage and challenge us to live boldly, and explain complicated or confusing Bible passages.

Show Pastor \_\_\_\_\_ how to equip us to walk in this world without being of this world. Let my pastor's messages fan into flame our faith so we are doers of the Word, not just hearers only (James 1:22). Amen

# DAY 18

## Bring People

Luke 12:31-33, *Do not be afraid, little flock, for your Father has been pleased to give you the kingdom.*

Heavenly Father, bring Pastor _____ the people You want to be in the church. Draw people through the doors who do not know You. Open their eyes and ears and spirits to the truth being presented. Tear down the walls that have kept them in darkness, and defeat the evil one and any hold it has on their lives. Let these who are lost, find a place that is welcoming and accepting of them, while offering them help, hope and healing in Your name. And give them the courage to respond to the invitation of salvation and commit their life to Christ.

Father, bring Pastor _____ people who belong to You but have wandered away from their faith, who are no longer hot, but lukewarm. Return to them the joy of their salvation! Revive their spirit with an outpouring of the Holy Spirit who will lift them up, inspire them and motivate them to live out their faith. Let them find a place that can restore their sense of awe in You, be led by the Holy Spirit, be strengthened in their faith, and learn about their spiritual gifts.

Father, bring Pastor _____ people who are mature in their faith and sold out to You! Encourage them to use their gifts to build the body here. Let them find a place of true worship, of maturing in the Word, and of fellowshipping with like-minded believers. Let them find people who will be their prayer partners, accountability partners, do life together, and be like iron sharpening iron, encouraging one another in their faith.

As these people come, let there be an environment of acceptance and sharing for mutual spiritual growth and friendship. Help everyone receive the encouragement they need to find their place in the body of Christ. Let their hearts, minds, and ears be opened to seek and hear from You. Amen

# DAY 19

## Hearing God

Isaiah 30:21, *Whether you turn to the right or to the left, your ears will hear a voice behind you, saying, "This is the way; walk in it."*

Heavenly Father, drown out the voices of the world, the flesh and the evil one that seek to distract and deceive Pastor _____. Those voices can cause fear, anger, confusion, discouragement, depression, and hopelessness. And even try and tempt them into all kinds of ungodly ideologies and behaviors.

Even my pastor's own inner voice may reflect self-doubt, self-criticism and insecurity. Father, silence those voices. Show my pastor that Your voice is loving and kind and does not condemn, but lifts up.

Like the sheep know the voice of their Shepherd let Pastor _____ become familiar with the sound of Your voice and be responsive to it. Teach them how to "tune in" to the many ways You speak. And open their spiritual ears to hear all You would say regarding their life, circumstances, relationships, and Your amazing, unconditional love.

Obviously, You speak through Your Word, the Holy Spirit, and in prayer. Remind Pastor _____ to seek other ways to hear You: dreams, visions, Your creation, open doors, circumstances, and blessings. Let them hear Your voice through other mature Christians speaking through books, podcasts, or everyday conversations. Let Pastor _____ also understand that You speak through closed doors, pain, and people who rub them the wrong way. Open my pastor's spiritual ears to what You have to say to them through any of these and help them understand You clearly.

Remind Pastor _____ that everything You say will agree with scripture, produce the fruit of the Spirit in their lives, and draw them closer to You. So let them listen carefully, and examine the results of their actions.

If Pastor _____ brings questions to You, answer them quickly whether the answer is yes, no, wait, or something entirely different, so they will not be left in confusion. Speak to Pastor _____ today about something that concerns them. When they feel overwhelmed by the world and all its noise, let them sense Your peace amidst the storm.

Strengthen Pastor _____ to listen and obey. Amen

# DAY 20

## Lifelong Mentoring

1 Corinthians 11:1, *Follow my example as I follow the example of Christ.*

Heavenly Father, send godly role models and mentors to Pastor \_\_\_\_\_ throughout their life. Bring those they respect, who they can watch, listen to, and learn from. It's so important for pastors to have someone they can bounce ideas off of, and be accountable to. Someone they can be honest with about the challenges and difficulties of being a pastor, marriage partner, and parent. Someone who will keep their confidence. And hold them accountable to their faith in all circumstances.

Let my pastor see other pastors and godly people making wise decisions based on a Biblical world view, and not being swayed by the marketing techniques, political opinions, and current philosophies of the world. Bring exactly who they need at different times of their life. Let Pastor \_\_\_\_\_ even learn from the mistakes of others to avoid making the same ones.

Let my pastor's mentor take an active interest in them and in their spiritual development, speaking Your truth and modeling how to live that truth in an ungodly world. It may be someone they already know. Or someone new they connect with.

Give this mentor opportunities to observe and speak into Pastor \_\_\_\_\_'s life on all kinds of issues: relational, financial, social, and spiritual. Give them Your wisdom to know how to interact with and be involved with Pastor \_\_\_\_\_ in a natural, relaxed way.

Create opportunities for my pastor and a mentor to have protected conversations about personal and spiritual issues. Let this mentor be a teacher, a guide, someone who by being connected to You, can give Pastor \_\_\_\_\_ consistent, sound wisdom from scripture.

Father, in this same way provide a mentoring relationship for my pastor's spouse. Perhaps another couple who has experience with and can understand ministry relationships. They would benefit from a mentoring relationship that can lead and guide them both through common trials and hardships that come from living with and loving someone in ministry.

Thank You for using role models and mentors for Your purposes in Pastor \_\_\_\_\_'s life. Amen

# DAY 21

# Wisdom

1 Kings 4:29-31, *God gave Solomon wisdom and very great insight, and a breadth of understanding as measureless as the sand on the seashore. Solomon's wisdom was greater than the wisdom of all the people ... wiser than anyone else... And his fame spread to all the surrounding nations.*

Heavenly Father, help Pastor _____ be like Solomon. He recognized the enormity of both the blessing and the responsibility You had given him as king. And in the face of this, and in humility, he asked for wisdom.

You have given my Pastor an incredible blessing of leading our church. It is easy to feel inadequate to fill so many needs. Alone, they cannot do it.

Pastor _____ is no doubt faced with opposing views and handling disagreements in the church. In a famous example of Solomon's wisdom, he discerned that the true mother of a living baby would give it up rather than see it destroyed (1 Kings 3:16-28).

Help my pastor see past the loudest voice or the squeakiest wheel to the heart of the matter at hand. Give them supernatural insight and wisdom to know truth. Show them the best way to bring Your wisdom and peace into all situations, whether small misunderstandings or larger disagreements.

You have promised to give wisdom generously to those who ask (James 1:5). So help my pastor ask for and receive the wisdom they need to act wisely. Show Pastor _____ the difference between the wisdom that comes from You and that which comes from other sources (James 3:13-17). There is a sense in our flesh and a logic of the mind that can lead us astray. And the philosophies of the world are rarely true wisdom. The devil even offers suggestions too. None of these serve Your purposes to bring godly direction and peace.

Give Pastor _____ a discerning heart when speaking and relating to people. Help them understand when to speak and when to be silent, to know what needs to be said, and be able to speak the truth in love.

Let Pastor _____ be attentive to Your voice and sensitive to Your working in their life, and in the lives of their family and our church. Help my pastor live in complete dependence on You for the wisdom and guidance necessary do Your will. Amen

## Reflections

Week 3! You are over halfway there! Great job!
We are really proud of you for making this commitment. Good for you! If you have missed any prayers, just pick up tomorrow where you left off. During your prayer time this week, has God shown you anything about Himself? About yourself? About your pastor?

_____

_____

If you know any specific needs your pastor or their family has, or if God brings something else to mind, make a note of it here and pray for it now or include it in next week's prayer time.

_____

_____

In thinking back over the prayers prayed this week...
→Since praying for your pastor's messages, consider writing a short note or card or send an email or text to your pastor sharing some way one of their messages has had an impact on your life. As you think of them, list some here.

_____

_____

→In asking God to bring people to your church, think about who you might invite to come. Jot their names down here. Invite one of those to attend this week.

_____

_____

→Consider how you hear God speaking yourself. If you aren't sure you're hearing from God, see Appendices F, G, and H on Hearing From God.
Note how you hear from God here. And what you have asked God about or heard from Him recently.

_____

_____

→Who are your role models or mentors? Are you a mentor to someone younger?

If you don't feel you have, or are being a mentor, maybe ask God to show you someone who could enter your life in this area. Some churches have mentor programs and you can connect there. Or there may be someone God shows you who you could approach and ask about this. It might be someone you respect and look up to, or some teen in the youth group who's interested in your field of work or a younger mom or dad who would benefit from your experience.
If anyone comes to mind, jot their name here and ask God to connect you for lunch in the near future to see if it would be a good match.

→In praying about wisdom, is there something in your life you need wisdom for? Those verses in the Day 21 prayer apply to you too. Ask God for wisdom, and He will give it. If you're unsure it's from Him, check it against scripture, what it will produce and how it affects your relationship with God in Appendix H on Hearing God Worksheet. Note here what you need wisdom for and write a simple prayer asking God to give you wisdom for that situation.

## *Halfway point check:*

Have you sensed any pushback?
> When you are praying intentionally and consistently, that does not make the evil one happy. You may sense pushback by finding yourself facing hardship or discouragement. Or there could be an upset with the church or pastor you're praying for, or any other relationship, or your work or home life. Maybe a sudden health issue or unexplained crisis. It may seem to come out of the blue, with no warning and no logic as to why things are happening.

Have you experienced anything like that? What?

_____

_____

_____

_____

If this happens, it could be spiritual, so it's helpful to be sure you are praying on Armor of God as part of your daily prayer time. Even a simple prayer like:
> Heavenly Father, thank You for the armor You give me that protects me as I pray. I put on the Helmet of Salvation to protect my mind, and the Breastplate of Righteousness as protection for my heart. I put on the Belt of Truth to help me discern truth and reject any lies. I wear the Shoes of the Gospel of Peace and take up the Shield of Faith and the Sword of the Spirit to fight in the battles You call me to.

> For more information see the Appendix B Spiritual Armor for Battle at the back of the book.

> And ask God to guard you and protect you, your family, your health, finances, relationships, home, job, and whatever else you feel led to pray about that could be attacked. Ask God to keep you standing firm.

> It also helps to talk with another Christian friend and ask them to pray for you and what you're experiencing. Or even for the duration of this 40 day journey.

Name anyone you might ask to pray for you, and anything you may have been experiencing. Consider writing a prayer here to ask for God's wisdom and protection for the rest of your 40 day journey.

# DAY 22
## Ephesians 3:14-21

Ephesians 3:16, *I pray that out of his glorious riches he may strengthen you...*

Heavenly Father, *I kneel before You*, the Creator of heaven and earth, and *pray that out of Your glorious riches*, far greater than we can even imagine, You *would strengthen* Pastor _____ *with power through Your Holy Spirit in their inner being*.

This is not a kind of might born of physical strength.

It is not intellectual acuity that results in a sense of superiority.

Or of the influence that comes from earthly measures of outward success.

When this happens, *Christ* truly *dwells within* Pastor _____ *'s heart* and they can live out their faith in Jesus.

*You have already given deep roots of faith and have securely established* Pastor _____ *in love*, because they have accepted Your gift of salvation. With this foundation, *I pray that* Pastor _____ *will be empowered to personally understand and be able to grasp*

*how wide and long and high and deep Christ's love is for them.*

And not with just a "head" knowledge, but to know and understand by experience, Your personal, unconditional love.

*And that* Pastor _____ *would acknowledge that Your love surpasses any other knowledge*—

of the flesh,

of the world,

and of the evil one.

In that knowledge they will *be filled with the fullness*, the richness of sensing Your presence more consistently in their life. A life more full *of You*.

Father, there is nothing beyond Your ability to do. In addition, You have the desire to act in my pastor's life to demonstrate Your love and power. I pray that *You will use this mighty power in* my pastor's life to answer not only the prayers they utter with their lips, but the ones they whisper with their heart, that only You hear, *in ways they cannot think to ask or even imagine.*

And let Pastor _____ know without a doubt that it is You at work within them. *And we will give You the glory due*—all the praise, all the honor, all our thanks, *forever and ever.* Amen

# DAY 23
## Time with You

Mark 6:30-31, *The apostles gathered around Jesus and reported to him all they had done and taught... he said to them, "Come with me by yourselves to a quiet place and get some rest."*

Heavenly Father, show Pastor _____ the blessing of time alone with You. Issue the same invitation You gave the disciples, *"Come with me."* And encourage them to simply spend quiet, uninterrupted, focused time with You.

Show them a place...maybe their office, a room at home, a coffee shop, a walk outside. Simple, relaxing places to focus on you. And how to schedule specific times set aside just for You.

Help my pastor be more aware of and thankful for who You are. Give them opportunities and let Pastor _____ stand in awe of You—with a reverence and respect for Your power, Your boundless creativity, Your ability to be everywhere at all times, and to know their mind, heart and every personal need.

And in spending time with You, show Pastor _____ how infinite Your love is for them, and all the ways You bless and care for them. Remind my pastor of Your faithfulness, how You have been there for them in ways that will strengthen their faith in You.

Give Pastor _____ a hunger and thirst for opportunities to pour out their heart, addressing every care and need they have in their personal or professional life, past, present or future. And for quietly listening for Your response, Your wisdom and direction, Your encouragement. Speak to Pastor _____ as only You can. Whether short or long; give them moments alone with You.

Father, let this become a regular pattern in their life. Any time with You is time well spent. Whether You answer a specific prayer, give a revelation about Yourself, or a fresh perspective on something, You can provide direction or encouragement for the path they're on.

Even if there is no new revelation, there is blessing for Pastor _____ in spending restful time with You, the Almighty Creator of the universe, and becoming aware of Your love for them and Your purpose for their life. Bless them as they make time for You. Amen

# DAY 24

# The Solution to a Problem

Jeremiah 33:3, *Call to me and I will answer you and tell you great and unsearchable things you do not know.*

Heavenly Father I ask that You would supernaturally provide the solution to a problem or issue that Pastor _____ is facing. Whether in the church or at home, whether financial or with a relationship, whether facing a decision or issue with their family, I know You have the answer that will help them. Lead my pastor to call on You, and reveal Your solution to them.

Often, with the stress of facing difficult decisions or problems, we have a limited perspective and only see solutions that are right in front of us. Father, give Pastor _____ a greater perspective, Your perspective.

Where they may only see choices A or B, open their eyes if You are presenting a totally new and unique answer. You can see options that are better solutions than anyone else could possibly think of or even imagine.

Father, move people, change circumstances, open or close doors that will show Pastor _____ that You are at work in their life to bring them answers to what concerns them. Delight my pastor by presenting them with the solution they need in such a way they have no doubt it has come from You.

Father, so many people speak into my pastor's life with their opinions. Illuminate the solution You are bringing to the table. And give them the courage to go forward with that solution. Amen

# DAY 25

## Committed Friends

Luke 5:18-19, *Some men came carrying a paralyzed man on a mat and tried to take him into the house to lay him before Jesus. When they could not find a way to do this because of the crowd, they went up on the roof and lowered him on his mat through the tiles into the middle of the crowd, right in front of Jesus.*

Heavenly Father, send Pastor _____ friends like these. They were aware of the need, and went to great lengths to help their friend, no matter the hardship. Their actions spoke volumes about their loyalty and the tight bonds they shared.

Bring a close group of loyal, committed friends who will spend enough time to be aware of Pastor _____'s needs. People they can speak honestly and openly with who will be trustworthy and keep confidences. People they can share joys and struggles with who will be discreet and are willing to think outside the box when necessary. And are willing to intercede for each other for godly wisdom on issues that arise in their friendships.

Grow an inner circle of committed friends who are willing to listen when my pastor needs to bounce ideas off someone, or be held accountable. People who would be fun to pal around with but also exhibit godly behavior, ask the hard questions, and aren't afraid to confront sin when they see it.

As this group develops, let them be able to speak into each other's lives. When needed, words of wisdom, guidance, comfort, correction and encouragement. And more than speak, be able to demonstrate their friendship by action, spending energy, attention, and resources on each other.

Thank You Father for bringing those who have been cheerleaders and supporters for Pastor _____. Thank You for the words of encouragement, gifts of time, support, and prayers from those You bring from time to time to reassure, inspire and cheer them on.

Pastor _____ also needs those loyal, committed friends who are in it for the long haul. Thank You for knowing in advance what Pastor _____ needs. And for protecting them from relationships that would be damaging or steer them in an ungodly direction. Thank You for providing those who would carry my pastor, should they need it. And who will be there for them through thick and thin. Amen

# DAY 26

## Courageous

Deuteronomy 31:6, *"Be strong and courageous. Do not be afraid or terrified because of them, for the Lord your God goes with you; he will never leave you nor forsake you."*

Heavenly Father, make Pastor _____ courageous. Don't let my pastor compare the size of any enemy to their own strength and be filled with fear and dread. Or spread that fear to others. But remind Pastor _____ to see the enemy they're facing compared to Your size and strength!

Your power, Your authority, and Your sovereignty far outweigh any other power on, above, or beneath the earth. And You have promised to always be at my pastor's side. Remind Pastor _____ that their ally is the Almighty Creator of the universe!

They need only call on You -
　　The One who can do miracles!
　　The One who keeps His promises!
　　The One who is faithful to His Word!

Do not let Pastor _____ listen to the voices of the world, or look at outward appearances. And do not let them listen to the voice of the enemy who wants to keep them fearful, discouraged and overwhelmed. Do not let fear get the better of my pastor, but help them seek out Your promises and hold to those even in the face of trials and trouble.

Show Pastor _____ that the future You have promised is exceedingly good—for them personally, and the big dreams You have given them for the church. Do not let them give up before the battle has even begun. Or let them focus on the challenges before them—instead of the ally standing beside them.

Help my pastor realize that when You are with them, there is no protection for the enemy. Lead Pastor _____ forward into the future You have for them and help them take possession of it, being strong and courageous. Amen

# DAY 27

## Vision

Habakkuk 2:2, *Write down the revelation and make it plain on tablets so that a herald may run with it.*

Heavenly Father, reveal Your vision to Pastor _____ for our church. For where we are now, and for what You have for our future. Grant them the ability to hear Your voice and see the direction we should go that will best glorify You in our community. Show them the best way to reach the people You are calling to be part of the ministry and mission You have for this church. Remind my pastor of the Call You have placed on their life, that You are always near, and that there is nothing too big that You can't empower them to accomplish.

Show Pastor _____ how to see through an eternal lens, not just a temporal one. Give my pastor the courage to trust You to do Your work in and through them and the church, and not try and make their own plans, then ask You to bless those plans.

**Internal**—Give Pastor _____ insight for how to have the church both meet the needs of, and use the gifts of the people You are calling to be members of the congregation. I lift up the Church Ministries my pastor needs Your vision for:

  Music ministry—Instruments -Equipment—Voices
  Prayer Teams—for Pastors—for services—during week—Partners
  Visitation—in homes—in Hospitals
  Discipleship/Bible Study
    Classes—Men—Women—Youth/Children-Singles
  Community Groups—Leaders—Locations—Curriculum
  Counseling—Marriage—Pre-marital—Leaders—Other
  Sunday School—Leaders—Curriculum
  Benevolence fund—Standards—Education—Support—Board
  Programs
    Parent's Night Out—MOPS—Special needs Buddy—Single Moms—Widows—Elderly—Church-wide events—Picnics—Hikes—Camping—Game night—Retreats

**Outreach**—As each community will be different. Remind Pastor \_\_\_\_\_ not to just do what they did at their last church, but take time to seek Your purpose for us in the community. I ask for Your vision for outreaches into our community:

- Christmas/Easter Services
- Music/Theatrical performances
- Trunk or Treat
- Food Drives
- Food Bank
- Thrift Store
- Celebrate Recovery
- Haven's Hope
- Clothing Drive
- Single Moms
- Youth sports
- Elderly

Global—Father, reveal to Pastor \_\_\_\_\_ what our footprint should look like in the world. Present a vision of mission organizations and missionaries our church could partner with. Or where there are people in our congregation who are already involved in long or short-term mission endeavors. Give our pastor a vision of where and how to provide financial or prayer support or participate with "boots on the ground" volunteers in areas of:

- World hunger
- Poverty
- Orphan adoption
- Sex trafficking
- Clean water
- Building projects
- Medical or
- Dental healthcare

Father, for each vision You give Pastor \_\_\_\_\_ bring the financial support in miraculous ways that we will know You are the one providing for it. Bring the volunteers and qualified people to be the manpower needed. Pave the way for plans to move forward. Even if there appear to be stumbling blocks or delays, remind us that Your purpose and Your timing are perfect. And that You will defeat the enemy with Your plans standing firm. Amen

# DAY 28

# Divine Appointments

Philippians 2:13, *For it is God who works in you to will and to act in order to fulfill his good purpose.*

Heavenly Father, give Pastor _____ "Divine Appointments". Arrange opportunities for them to be in the right place at the right time to hear or see something or someone who will contribute to Your provision for their life, their family or their ministry.

Orchestrate meetings with other people who can bless them, or introduce them to the answers they're looking for or the connections they need. Even if only a momentary influence in their life, let these happenings occur often. Create a constant stream of positive, godly direction for Pastor _____.

Help Pastor _____ discern when something is an interruption distracting them from Your purpose or what needs to be done, and when it is a Divine Appointment meant for them, from You. Heavenly Father, You created the universe! Let my pastor witness events or casual occurrences that make a connection with You, Your power and Your purpose. And when they do, give them clarity to focus on what's happening, and make time for it.

Whether in a podcast, the theme of a movie or a real-life situation, that gives them an example for a sermon, or the right person to be on staff, or the right outreach for the church, let them see You in a way that connects with something that You are teaching them.

When happening, open Pastor _____'s mind and heart and spirit to the influences You bring their way.

Father, work in Pastor _____'s life in new and unexpected ways that surprise and delight them, and meet their needs. Amen

## *Reflections*

Week 4! AMAZING JOB!
We are really proud of you and you are on the right track!
If you have missed any prayers, just pick up tomorrow where you left off.
During your prayer time this week, has God shown you anything about Himself? About yourself? About your pastor?

_____

_____


If you know any specific needs your pastor or their family has, or if God brings something else to mind, make a note of it here and pray for it now or include it in next week's prayer time.

_____

_____


→ Consider writing a short note or card or send an email or text to let your pastor know you've been praying for them to have positive time alone with God, to gain a solution to a problem, have committed friendships, courage, and that God would provide them with a vision and Divine Appointments that will connect them with God's plan for them and for the church. Ask if there have been examples of answers to your group's prayers they can share?

In thinking back over the prayers prayed this week...
→ Our Heavenly Father is also inviting you to "Come with Me." If it's been a while since you had personal quiet time, schedule some time to simply sit with the Lord. Pour out your heart with all that is going on in your life. Ask Him to speak to your issues, remind you of His love for

you, show you answers, solutions, the next step for the path you're on. Sometimes it is encouraging to write down what you are speaking to God about so you can be on the lookout for the answers He provides. Feel free to list some of those things here.

_____

_____

_____

→If you need a solution to a problem, pray Day 24 prayer for yourself, asking God to reveal a solution from His perspective. Note it here and then see how God provides an answer.

_____

_____

→If your pastor has had a vision for any programs, needs or projects being planned or going on at this time, pray for those. List them here, and pray about any way you might fit in to serve your pastor or your church in areas of upcoming projects or ministries.

_____

_____

→Consider making a call to the appropriate staff or volunteer person heading up the area you might be interested in. Get any details that will help you pray for them and pray about offering your time, energy or finances to help out.
Who will you call? About what? How might you help?

_____

_____

_____

# DAY 29

## Psalm 20:1-9

Psalm 20:1, *May the Lord answer you when you are in distress...*

O Lord, answer Pastor _____ when they are in distress. Remind them to call out to You, and let them hear Your voice above all else. You are never too busy to hear Pastor _____'s cry for help. Thank You that You can handle any kind of distress possible.

Regardless of the situation You can help. Whether in anxiety, fear, depression, or grief, You can handle it. If there is spiritual turmoil, confusion, or my pastor is feeling tempted, deliver them.

*May the name of the God of Jacob protect* Pastor _____'s life, health, relationships, mind, emotions, and spirit. There is great power in Your name. Yahweh! Jehovah! Jesus! Almighty God! Adonai!

*May You send* Pastor _____ *help from the sanctuary* where You sit enthroned and have angels as Your messengers doing Your bidding, *and grant support from Zion*. You can reach my pastor with just the help they need. Your help is better than any the world can offer. You deliver them and help them bear up under any circumstance or oppression.

*May You remember all* my pastor's *sacrifices and accept their burnt offerings.* The sacrifices You desire are obedience and a contrite or repentant heart. May Pastor _____'s life be entirely and wholly offered to You. May their words, actions, and attitudes all honor You.

*May You give* Pastor _____ *the desires of their heart* and remove any desires that would not honor You. *And make all their plans succeed* as You direct their steps.

*Some trust in chariots and some in horses, but* Pastor _____ *trusts in the name of the Lord their God.* The power and might of the world are worthless compared to Yours. Pastor _____ does not place their trust in world leaders, politicians, athletes, or any other person of influence. They do not find their sense of security in money, fame, position, good looks, or good health. But they trust in You alone.

*We will shout for joy when* Pastor _____ *is victorious and will lift up our banners in the name of our God!* Amen!

# DAY 30

## Spiritual Power

Psalm 3:1, 3, LORD, *how many are my foes! How many rise up against me!*
*But you, LORD, are a shield around me, my glory, the One who lifts my head high.*

Heavenly Father, stand with Pastor _____ when they are facing any enemy. There is no doubt that You involve Yourself with spiritual circumstances here on earth. And intercede to bring about Your purposes.

Thank You that I am assured that You know what will come next in Pastor _____'s life, and will prepare and empower them for it, encourage them through it, and cause things to work together for their good.

No matter how many are against Pastor _____, You are a shield around them. You protect my pastor from the attack; repelling arrows, stopping fiery darts, deflecting blows. Pastor _____ can stand safely behind You and the Shield of Faith You supply believers.

Not a flimsy garbage can lid, but a battle shield: reaching from head to toe and covering side to side. When standing next to another, the shields meet and form a wall. This shield is thick enough to prevent penetration by darts or arrows. And shiny to reflect the sun, blinding the enemy.

Pastor _____ can take up the Sword of the Spirit and with Your powerful words from scripture, cut the enemy to ribbons. For demons believe in You, and tremble at Your power (James 2:19). Your Word overcomes any lies the evil one uses to distract, confuse or entrap my pastor.

You have ways to fight for Pastor _____ we haven't even imagined. And when they cannot mount their own defense, You are there, protecting and sustaining them. Thank You that no weapon formed against Pastor _____ can stand (Isaiah 54:17). And thank You that You fight for Pastor _____ against their enemies and give them victory (Deuteronomy 20:4).

So do not let my pastor fear—even when they see the enemy drawn up against them. Whether it's worldly lies, sexual temptations, financial worries or health concerns, fill them with Your power! And deliver them!

Thank You Father for Your immeasurable love, and for Your almighty power which You use to strike down Pastor _____'s enemies. All praise to You! Amen

# DAY 31

## Unity of Staff

Romans 12:4-5, *For just as each of us has one body with many members, and these members do not all have the same function, so in Christ we, though many, form one body, and each member belongs to all the others.*

Heavenly Father, organize a staff around Pastor _____ who will support them and the church. No one person can do all the tasks it takes to run a church and all the ministries that happen on a daily and weekly basis. So bring capable, ethical, people who have the gifts, talents and abilities that are needed to do the work.

Allow each person on staff the freedom to operate in the gifts and strengths You have given them, mindful of the responsibilities that come with the job they're doing. Blend the personalities to be able to work together to accomplish meeting the needs of the church and its members. Help them work as a team, in unity to meet any challenge. And when disagreements occur, give everyone a measure of grace to work together and arrive at what's best for the church, putting personal preferences aside.

There may be naturally occurring disconnects between the office staff and the preaching, teaching or music people on staff. Help Pastor _____ create a culture of connectivity among all. Every person is needed, so make it a priority that every person on staff is valued. Whether vacuuming the halls, paying the bills, scheduling Sunday School teachers, leading the Youth, or preaching the weekly message, all are valued parts of the body. Help my pastor see to it that all are heard in meetings, and the needs are appropriately met for all to operate smoothly.

Teach Pastor _____ how to plan team building, retreats, and fun activities to support friendships, so when issues come up there's an underlying level of trust, unity, and desire to work together.

Help Pastor _____ find a balance where they are not detached from the needs of the staff, but are also not over-involved or micro-managing their people. Show when to delegate and how to pick the right person for the job that fits their strengths. Create a willingness for staff to step up when needed. And when big projects come up, help Pastor _____ explain in a way that others catch the vision too, to understand and support the work that needs to be done.

Let the running of our church be a joy-filled team effort. Amen

# DAY 32

## Encouragement

Joshua 1:9, *Have I not commanded you? Be strong and courageous. Do not be afraid; do not be discouraged, for the L*ORD *your God will be with you wherever you go.*

Heavenly Father, bring the emotional and spiritual encouragement and support that Pastor _____ needs to deal with daily challenges and more difficult burdens that arise.

Fill my pastor with the motivation and direction they need to meet whatever lies before them in order to be energized to go on mentally, emotionally and spiritually. Remind them You are with them always, and let that strong sense of Your presence fill them with strength and courage.

You created Pastor _____. And You knew beforehand the purpose of their life, the places they would go, and the perils they would face. You carefully fashioned and have prepared them to handle, with Your help, whatever they need to face now. Show them the confidence, faith, and tools You have already built into them to be more than a conqueror.

Bring whatever encouragement Pastor _____ needs in the moment: a new perspective, another person to help with the load, a word from a friend, a beautiful sunset. Let my pastor hear truth from Your Word, or recall scriptures that reinforce Your love and support for them. Your promises are personal:

> You have carried Pastor _____ since their birth…You will continue to be with Pastor _____ and sustain them, even when they have gray hairs. You will always carry Pastor _____; You will always sustain Pastor _____; You will always rescue Pastor _____ (Isaiah 46:3-4).
>
> You are with Pastor _____ always. You will always be holding their hand; You will guide Pastor _____ with Your counsel, and take them into glory…You are the strength of Pastor _____'s heart and their portion forever (Psalm 73:23-26).

Recall to my pastor how You were faithful to them in the past. Let those memories strengthen and build their faith. And let Pastor _____ observe courage in others facing similar challenges and learn from those mistakes and triumphs.

Let my pastor rest assured that You will do Your part. And be encouraged to keep going. Amen

# DAY 33

## Coping with trials

John 16:33, *"I have told you these things, so that in me you may have peace. In this world you will have trouble. But take heart! I have overcome the world."*

Heavenly Father, Thank You for helping Pastor _____ cope with trials. Pastors are subject to the same things that happen to everyone. They experience the same interruptions in their day that we do: backed up sinks, car trouble, sick children. Things that interrupt their day and need to be dealt with urgently.

Another level of circumstances completely derail us: a serious accident, a grim diagnosis, a miscarriage. Father, be by Pastor _____'s side in real and tangible ways they can see and feel when these things happen. Protect them from the devastating results by being their hope and support. Just like us, there are times when it seems nothing is going right, and never will. Send them help from Your sanctuary; angels to meet their needs and protect them during the challenging times of coping with hardship.

We also struggle with relationships from time to time. Even more so for a pastor who deals with so many people beyond the normal family and friends. Because their workplace is a church, pastors are expected to get along with staff more than the usual job site. And even more, pastors are asked to relate to and serve the members of the church. That can be hundreds of people who all have opinions and needs that can be time consuming and emotionally draining.

In addition to the circumstances and relationships, there are internal struggles we all face. Father, help Pastor _____ when they are dealing with unmet expectations, unfulfilled hopes, personal issues that leave them feeling weary or confused. Father, in Your faithfulness, give Pastor _____ strength: mentally, emotionally, and spiritually. Remind them that all these things are in Your capable hands, and nothing is beyond Your help.

Let Pastor _____ breathe in Your peace, and breathe out praises and thanks, even in the midst of trials. Deliver the help they need, whatever form that may take. Grant them the desires of their heart. And give them success as they follow through in Your plans for their life and their ministry. Amen

# DAY 34

## Property

Matthew 18:21, *For where two or three are gathered in my name, there I am with them.*

Heavenly Father, let Pastor _____ lead our church to be a light in the community. Let the place we worship be welcoming, whether a freestanding building, part of a shopping mall, a shared-use facility, on a military base, or in someone's home. May we be a noticeable and beneficial presence - a sweet fragrance of You to a world in need of a Savior.

Give Pastor _____ a clear vision for our location and the work You plan for our church. Encourage their work with the city and other faith-based organizations to ensure our church has good connections and can bloom where we're planted. And if the opportunity comes to relocate, purchase land or build in a new location, guide Pastor _____ in how to make that decision.

Lead Pastor _____ to trustworthy people who are smart with money and skilled dealing with church finances, budget planning, and even building projects, should You lead us to future building improvements or construction.

Anoint our property with the Holy Spirit. From the time people drive onto it, let Your presence be felt. Make our signs visible so that everyone who passes by sees we are a church and thinks of You; raising questions about eternity and salvation and about who the Lord Jesus Christ really is. Spark in them a thirst to know more, a desire to check out our services, events, and The Bible.

Keep our property safe from vandalism and forces of nature that might destroy or deface it. Send angels to surround the property and protect everyone who visits, and from the evil one's attempts to block them from the truth.

Let every car and pedestrian be safe while moving and when parked. Keep the parking lot free from accidents, violence, drug deals and evil intentions. Turn away every evil power that would seek to harm or harass anyone on our property.

Let our property be a place where both believers and the community can gather and experience Your presence and Your power. Amen

# DAY 35

## Building

Proverbs 24:3-4, *By wisdom a house is built, and through understanding it is established; through knowledge its rooms are filled with rare and beautiful treasures.*

Heavenly Father, bless Pastor _____ with church buildings that will meet the needs of the purposes You have for our church. Bless the walls, ceiling, roof and floors, windows and doors.

Allow for all maintenance needs, repairs, and upkeep of our facilities to be taken care of with tithes, offerings and financial gifts. Bring honest, reputable workers when repairs or improvements are needed. Whether the parking lot, the plumbing, electrical, heating or air conditioning, windows, carpet, painting or the bathrooms, let repairs be done in a timely manner. Bring volunteers to join in when appropriate and provide for persons with expertise to oversee any work.

If there is a church kitchen, keep the appliances running smoothly, and keep those who use it accountable to keep it clean and supplied. If there's a bookstore, bring a manager who will create the opportunity for people to get books and music that support Biblical values, inspire godly ideas and encourage their faith walk. If there is a reading room or prayer room, bring someone who will keep it secure, and stocked with shelves of godly resource material and comfortable seating.

If the church owns and operates cars, vans or buses, bless them and keep them in good running order, providing the finances and specialists who can deliver those services. Place a wall of protection around the drivers and vehicles when transporting people to or from church services, events, camps or retreats.

As the community or other churches need places for weddings, funerals, Scout troops, Commencements, or other occasions, let our pastor prayerfully consider the use of what You have given us to serve and bless the community. Let the people who use the building be diligent to care for it, clean it, and lock it.

Let every word spoken, every action taken honor You. Subdue and drive out any evil from our building. More than just a building, let our property be a place of welcome and sanctuary for people of all ages to find their way to You. Amen

## Reflections

You are almost there!! Way to go!
You have come so far. And we are really proud of you!
If you have missed any prayers, just pick up tomorrow where you left off.
During your prayer time this week, has God shown you anything about Himself? About yourself? About your pastor?

_____

_____


If you know any specific needs your pastor or their family has, or if God brings something else to mind, make a note of it here and pray for it now or include it in next week's prayer time.

_____


In thinking back over the prayers prayed this week...

→Just like you prayed for your pastor on Day 30, God has promised to be your Shield as well. If you are facing something difficult, bring that specifically to God's attention in prayer.
Put on your spiritual armor and ask God to dispel the attack you are feeling. Take up your Shield of Faith and rest behind it if you need to. Or use it to press forward against the enemy. Use the Sword of the Spirit and speak scripture and the name of the Lord Jesus Christ to attack and repel the enemy. List any scriptures that will encourage you or help you remember how powerful God is.

_____

_____

_____

_____

→Consider writing a short note or card or send an email or text of appreciation to one or more of your church staff. You could include a scripture you prayed this week or just let them know that you notice the work they do and appreciate it. Name who you will contact.

_____

→You prayed for encouragement for your pastor on Day 32. What encourages you?

_____
_____


Consider doing something this week that will encourage your pastor. It could be a word of encouragement, a plate of cookies, an act of service, a coupon, gift, or donation...ask God to bring something to mind.

_____
_____


→If you know of any issues going on with your church property or buildings, furnishings or equipment, list them and pray about those specifically.
If there is a need you could potentially meet, put a check mark by those and consider donating your time, labor, skills, or money to help. Contact the pastor or staff person in charge of that area to get more information to see how you might help.

_____
_____
_____
_____
_____

# DAY 36

# Psalm 27:1-3, 5-8, 11-14

Psalm 27:1, *The Lord is my light and my salvation, whom shall I fear*

The LORD is Pastor \_\_\_\_\_'s light and their salvation; whom shall they fear? *The LORD is the stronghold of* my pastor's *life; of whom shall they be afraid?*

*When the wicked advance against* them, *to devour* them, *it is* my pastor's *enemies and foes who shall stumble and fall.*

*Though an army besiege* them, their *heart will not fear; though war break out against* them, *even then* they *will be confident.*

*For in the day of trouble he will keep* Pastor \_\_\_\_\_ *safe in his dwelling; he will hide* my pastor *in the shelter of his sacred tent, and set* them *high upon a rock.*

*Then* their *head will be exalted above the enemies who surround* them; *at his sacred tent* Pastor \_\_\_\_\_ *will sacrifice with shouts of joy;*
My pastor *will sing and make melody to the LORD.*

*Hear* my pastor's *voice when* they *call LORD; be merciful and answer* them.
My pastor's *heart says of you, "Seek his face!"*
*"Your face, LORD, I will seek."*

Teach my pastor *your way, LORD; lead* them *in a straight path because of* their *oppressors.*

*Do not turn* them *over to the desire of* their *foes, for false witnesses rise up against* my pastor, *spouting malicious accusations.*

*I remain confident of this:* Pastor \_\_\_\_\_ *will see the goodness of the Lord in the land of the living.*

*Wait for the LORD,* Pastor \_\_\_\_\_; *be strong, and take heart and wait for the LORD!*

DAY 37

## Congregation

Ephesians 4:14-16, *Then we will no longer be infants...blown here and there by every wind of teaching and by the cunning and craftiness of people in their deceitful scheming. Instead... we will grow to become in every respect the mature body of him who is the head, that is, Christ... joined and held together... as each part does its work.*

Heavenly Father, bless Pastor _____ with people who are willing to call our church their home. Bring those who are willing to serve and give of their time, energy, finances, talents, abilities and spiritual gifts to

build and strengthen this church body. And help my pastor communicate to us an understanding of the many and varied opportunities for serving that are needed to keep the church running and healthy.

Father, bring enough people that the needs of the ministries and mundane tasks of the church are met. Pastor _____ needs people who are willing to take responsibility for long term as well as one-time or short-term roles. Rather than seeing church as a country club to join and focus on being served, let our congregation see the church as a team to join and play their part.

Bring those who will show up and say, "Put me in, Coach!" and who will be ready to be the hands and feet, shoulders and knees Pastor _____ needs to move the ministry forward on a daily and weekly basis.

Father, fill our congregation with those who have gifts and talents for the music ministry and people to run the AV and technical side of services whether onsite or broadcasting to reach those in other places or at home.

Bring those who can teach to volunteer for Sunday School classes, Bible Studies, and Discipleship. Teachers have such a huge impact on people's lives, from children through adults. Bring those who love and can care for the babies and young children. And those who can step in when regular workers are sick or on vacation.

For every service draw volunteers to help with simple, even thankless tasks that are needed: direct parking, greet, hand out bulletins, make coffee, set up the sanctuary, and provide security. Bring people who can help during the week to do mailings, prepare classrooms, wash toys and nursery bedding, and be sure there are sufficient coffee cups and filters, napkins, and toilet paper.

Raise up people who will make and take meals, visit hospitals, work on church and outreach events. Anoint some to serve on prayer teams, for the pastor, staff, congregation, and for Your direction for the church in the community and in the world.

Father, let our congregation be a mix of young and old, families and singles, from different backgrounds, who come together to worship and serve with their gifts. From the oldest to the youngest, call people who are willing to be mentored by more mature believers, and also be role models and mentors for others newer in the faith.

Unity is a gift from You, Father. Let this body grow together, enjoying a unity of spirit and a vision for Your purpose that they are willing to support with their time, talents, and finances. Bless each volunteer richly for serving.

Grow us up in love. Bless Pastor _____ with a congregation where each one has a part to play, and each one plays their part. All for Your glory. Amen

# DAY 38

## Confidence

Jeremiah 17:7, *"But blessed is the one who trusts in the Lord, whose confidence is in him.*

Heavenly Father, there are times Pastor _____ may feel like the underdog. When they are overwhelmed give them confidence to take on the enemies they face.

When they come up against trouble:

1. Help Pastor _____ look beyond their own limitations and be confident in Your perspective.

    Looking only at ourselves limits the scope of solutions we can see and perform. Like David facing Goliath, if You have called my pastor to a battle, You are in the fight with them. And they need not fear. The battle is Yours.

2. Help Pastor _____ trust that You have already prepared them for the battle.

    Show Pastor _____ how to use the spiritual gifts, talents, abilities and experiences You have given them instead of feeling they need to conform to what others expect of them. Give them confidence Your preparation.

3. Let Pastor _____ voice confidence in You, giving You the glory for the victory even before it happens!

Father, let Pastor _____'s fear diminish and their faith grow!

Help Pastor _____ look beyond their own abilities to all You can do in and with and through them. Let them trust in Your preparation and Your purposefulness for their life. And in Your victory! Amen

# DAY 39

## Teachable

Proverbs 3:5-6, *Trust in the LORD with all your heart and lean not on your own understanding; in all your ways submit to him, and he will make your paths straight.*

Heavenly Father, Pastor _____'s life has the potential of being full of change. A new job, new church, location, meeting new people. Families change as children grow and parents age. And the needs of the church may change as well.

Thank You that you are with Pastor _____ in every change they go through. Thank You that You help my pastor learn how to live and cope with differing physical, emotional and social environments and in the midst of it all, teach them how to live a godly life.

You have promised to teach us the way we should go (Psalm 32:8). Although not usually in sky writing, and not recently through a burning bush, You connect with people in so many ways. Let my pastor hear all You have to teach them about how You prepare Pastor _____ for the work You call them to.

Help Pastor _____ be open to learn new things, and unlearn some things they thought they knew, by being open to the Holy Spirit. Let my pastor see clearly how You direct their path personally, and for their ministry.

Teach Pastor _____ how to interact best with those around them; both their inner circle, and those they interact with as pastor. When they make mistakes, thank You for the reassurance that You don't waste anything and are able to help us all learn from our mistakes.

Even as my pastor ages, gray hair often gives a sense of wisdom, experience and credibility, but losing hair is not the same. Teach Pastor _____ to cope with all life's changes and stay inspired and invigorated. Help them be open to whatever changes You allow.

Whether in relationships, finances, career, health, family, ministry, don't let Pastor _____ lean on their own understanding. Keep them open and teachable in making decisions and reacting to hardship and challenges.

In all circumstances, remind Pastor _____ to seek Your instruction, be open to Your direction, and to trust You with all their heart. Amen

DAY 40

# Aaronic Blessing: Numbers 6:24-26

Numbers 6:24, *The Lord bless you and keep you...*

Heavenly Father, as Aaron, the High Priest, gave this blessing over the people of Israel, I pray it now over Pastor _____. Defining the six Hebrew verbs adds a deeper understanding of the blessing's meaning. These expanded definitions come from Bill Bullock, The Rabbi's Son. Find him on www.biblicallifestylecenter.org

May You, Lord God, the Holy One, infuse Pastor _____ with unlimited potential and power and release them from any restrictions or limitations that would prevent them from reaching the fullness of their potential to participate in their divine purpose which You have given them.

May You zealously cherish and treasure Pastor _____, diligently defending and keeping watch over them to protect and save them.

May the light of Your innermost being and essence illuminate Pastor _____ physiologically and spiritually, impacting their body, mind, soul and spirit with Your warming, healing, soothing, restorative, empowering and constantly renewing energy.

May You, the Holy One, give Pastor _____ what they really need, not because they've earned it, or out of pity, benevolence, or even generosity, but because You have promised, as the stronger covenant partner, to strengthen Pastor _____ and enable them to reach their potential and enjoy the covenant You entered into with them, when they accepted You as Savior.

As You were face to face with the High Priest in the Holy of Holies, may You be present with Pastor _____ so they can experience true spiritual reality.

And may You place in and establish in Pastor _____, wholeness, wellness, purposeful living in joy, with abundant provision, harmony, safety, security summed up in the Hebrew word "Shalom" translated "peace." Amen

# THE "PRIESTLY BLESSING"

Y'varechecha Adonai
[May the Holy One bless you]
v'yish'merecha
[and zealously cherish and keep watch over you]
Ya'er Adonai panav elecha
[May the Holy One's Face shine upon you]
v'chuneka
[and shower you with grace]
Yisa Adonai panav elecha
[May the Holy One lift up His countenance upon you]
v'yasem lecha shalom
[and may He give you wholeness, wellness, security, abundant provision, and peace].
[Numbers 6:24-26]

# Reflections

CONGRATULATIONS!! You made it!!
You finished the work you started! You did it! The whole 40 days!
We are so proud of you!! How does it feel?

_____

In thinking back over the prayers prayed this week...
➙ No church is perfect because they are made up of imperfect people. Thinking about your congregation, if you know of any dissention among groups, pray for unity now. Ask God to speak directly to those involved in any situations that have caused division or problems for the church.
And ask God to show you if there is any way you might be part of a solution.

_____

➙ Consider writing a short note or card or send an email or text to your pastor to let them know you've completed your goal of 40 Days of Prayer for them! Perhaps include the Priestly Blessing for them.
And Maybe ask your Pastor to share their own thoughts from the last 40 days – things they've noticed while you or your group was praying for them. Any specific examples?
During your 40 day prayer journey, has God shown you anything new about Himself? How will you apply that to your life?

_____

_____

Have you learned anything about the one you prayed for? Will that change the way you think about them or interact with them?

_____

_____

_____

Has God shown you anything new about yourself?

_____

_____


Do you feel any differently about prayer?
Or about the way God works in others?
In you?

_____

_____


→ Have a time of Thanksgiving!
Write a prayer here, or list specific blessings or highlights of ways you've seen God work in your life during these 40 days—or this last year.

_____

_____

_____

_____


→ Is there another pastor you can pray these 40 days for now? Or is there another 40 Day Prayer Guide that will bless someone else? Or even yourself?
Praying for Someone's Salvation
Praying a Blessing for Someone
Praying for Godly Character
Praying for Your Grandchild

→ The verses you've prayed here are not just for pastors. Look back through the prayers and if there are areas that would benefit your own life, pray those for yourself and your family. Perhaps pray another 40 days for you!

→ Consider choosing some scriptures and some things to pray about and make your own 40 Day Prayer Journey!

## AFTERWARDS
# Thank You After 40 Days

Heavenly Father, thank You for this journey of praying intentionally and consistently for these 40 days. Thank You for Your promise to hear me when I call to You and answer my prayers. Do not let me forget the things I have learned about You, about prayer and about myself in these 40 days.

I pray that through these prayers Your power will be released in Pastor _____'s life. And that You will make Your presence known and Your blessings felt in their life. That Pastor _____ will sense You at work, in large ways and in small ones.

I am continually grateful that I can pray for You to bring about Your will and Your purpose in my pastor's life. I ask for You to demonstrate to Pastor _____ that through Your call on them You came to bring them an abundant life!

May Pastor _____ never ever forget that You are with them and that they are Your child. May that remembrance be a powerful deterrent and an awesome reassurance.

I believe Your Word will not return void, and as I have prayed Your Word and Your blessing over Pastor _____ I believe that it will continue to bear fruit long after these 40 days have passed.

Thank You for hearing and answering my prayers—in ways that are above and beyond what I could ever ask for or even imagine. Show me if there is someone else I can pray these prayers for...even for myself. Or if there is another 40 Day Prayer Guide that will bless someone else in my life. And be with me on that journey as well.

I give You my thanks and my praise! Amen

# APPENDICES

# APPENDIX A
# Confession and Repentance

Let God speak to you now and show you any sin you need to confess. Psalm 66:18 tells us if we cherish sin in our hearts, God won't listen to our prayers. Tell God you are willing to turn away from those things (which is repentance) and ask for His forgiveness.

1 John 1:9-10 tells us "If we confess our sins, He is faithful and righteous to forgive us our sins and to cleanse us from all unrighteousness. If we claim we have not sinned, we make Him a liar, and His word is not in us."

Ask God if there are sins of:

**THOUGHT**—impure, selfish, angry, fearful, jealous

**ATTITUDE**—prideful, judgmental, argumentative, lukewarm toward God

**SPEECH**—crude, inappropriate, grumbling, divisive, lies, half-truths

**RELATIONSHIP**—wrong or improper, physically or emotionally

    Do you need to forgive someone? Do you need to ask for forgiveness?

    As a husband: are you providing spiritual leadership, guiding and nurturing your wife?

    As a wife: are you honoring and respecting your husband?

    As parents: are you modeling godly behavior and attitudes and teaching your children in love?

    As children or teens: are you respectful and obedient?

**COMMISSION**—things that you have done, actions you have taken

    Have you done something you know is wrong?

    Do you guard your eyes?

    Have you exposed yourself to the occult?

    Do you have habits that are harmful to your body, mind, spirit?

**OMISSION**—things you have failed to do

    Has God prompted you to do something you haven't done?

    Have you failed to do good when you could have?

**SELF-RULE**—rebellion, going your own way

    Are you following God or going your own way?

    Are you avoiding something He's told you to do?

    Or are you still doing something He's told you not to?

# APPENDIX B

## Spiritual Armor for Battle

Ephesians 6:10-18, *Finally, be strong in the Lord and in his mighty power. Put on the full armor of God, so that you can take your stand against the devil's schemes. For our struggle is not against flesh and blood, but against the rulers, against the authorities, against the powers of this dark world and against the spiritual forces of evil in the heavenly realms. Therefore put on the full armor of God, so that when the day of evil comes, you may be able to stand your ground, and after you have done everything, to stand. Stand firm then, with the belt of truth buckled around your waist, with the breastplate of righteousness in place, and with your feet fitted with the readiness that comes from the gospel of peace. In addition to all this, take up the shield of faith, with which you can extinguish all the flaming arrows of the evil one. Take the helmet of salvation and the sword of the Spirit, which is the word of God.*

*And pray in the Spirit on all occasions with all kinds of prayers and requests. With this in mind, be alert and always keep on praying for all the Lord's people.*

We dress ourselves in the armor that Paul describes here. He wrote his letter to the Ephesians while he was in Rome, under house arrest, guarded by Roman soldiers. Every day, he saw men dressed in armor, bearing the insignia of their authority. The Holy Spirit must have inspired his analogy of a Christian "soldier."

**Praying on the armor can be as simple as listing each piece and stating that you are putting it on and wearing it.**

When we are praying for someone, or even ourselves, the devil doesn't like it. And even with his limited power here on earth, we can find ourselves under attack in ways that can lead us to feel discouraged, defeated, even want to give up.

But we rely on the fact that God's armor is the very best!

The **Belt of Truth** is a wide, tight band around the waist that holds pieces of the armor on as well as the sword. It provides support for the back and core. When we are "girded" with truth we can more easily recognize the lies the devil would tempt us to believe. We will not be mesmerized by half-truths or deceptions.

The **Breastplate of Righteousness** protects our heart and vital organs, a kind of forerunner of the bulletproof vest. It stops and deflects stabs and projectiles, keeping our heart and spirit from evil deceptions. Our righteousness comes from Jesus Christ. His blood paid the price for our sin and we gain the righteousness of the perfect life He lived. In that righteousness the devil cannot hold anything against us.

The **Shoes of the Gospel of Peace** help us walk in the Spirit. Putting on shoes is a sign of readiness and preparedness. With these we are ready to carry the Good News of salvation and peace into our relationships and whatever challenges we face. With our feet protected like this we will have traction even when we feel unsteady, and will be able to stand firm.

The **Shield of Faith** is not some puny little garbage can lid with a handle, but a head-to-toe protection, repelling the enemy's offensive weapons. When the shield was anointed with oil it would reflect the glare of the sun and blind the enemy. This shield covered a soldier from top to bottom, side to side and could join with others to form a wall of protection that would fend off an attacker while advancing in the field of battle.

Our faith in God protects us when the world or others tell us things are hopeless or cannot work out because we have the One True God who is all-knowing and all-powerful. We trust in His love for us and know that He has a plan for us, to give us hope and a future with Him in eternity. Every time He keeps a promise, or delivers us from some trouble, or stands with us in hardship, it builds our faith—strengthens our shields! And when we stand beside other believers in their faith, we are protected even more! And can move against the enemy.

The **Helmet of Salvation** protects our head and identifies who we fight for. This helmet also protects our minds and helps guard our thoughts. The enemy would want to fill our minds with thoughts of doubt, fear and insecurity. But when thoughts and emotional responses are stirred up, we can hold them up to the light of truth: scripture. God's Word is the truth that will combat all that would discourage us. So we take every thought captive, and if false, replace it with God's Word.

And the **Sword of the Spirit** is God's Word, and strikes at the lies the devil would use to try and defeat us. We can use it to refute any lies the devil tries to get us to believe. We can pray it as part of our prayers. We can speak it out loud as an attack on the enemy. The enemy trembles because there is power in the Word of God.

Here is a sample prayer:

Heavenly Father, I come before You with thanks for the armor that You give me, which is the best. With the Belt of Truth fastened around my waist, I say that I will not believe the lies the devil would try to use to confuse me. Give me clarity and understanding. Help me see past what the world and others would tell me, to what You want to say to me.

I place the Helmet of Salvation on my head to guard and guide my mind, and I take every thought captive to You. The Breastplate of Righteousness I put over my chest to protect my heart.

I wear the Shoes of the Gospel of Peace to say that I am ready to hear from You and obey what You tell me to do, and will follow where You lead. Light my path so I can know the way to go.

I take up my Shield of Faith to repel all the arguments and attacks the evil one sends against me. And I take up the Sword of the Sprit, the Word of God, as a weapon to help me fight and stand firm against the devil's schemes.

Go with me into battle, and give me victory! Amen

# APPENDIX C
# Prayer for Military Chaplains

Oh Father, in addition to caring for a congregation, seeking out the lost, preaching a word, and providing counseling in an ungodly world, this man or woman has been called to put their very lives on the line. They may find themselves in combat situations where literally life and death are the main concerns.

Military Chaplains not only stand in the pulpit, but stand in the foxholes. They not only worship in the Chapel, but worship on the war field. They not only march in parades, but march into battle.

Father protect these brave men and women who have heard and accepted Your Calling on their lives. Honor them with Your gift of long life. Help them sense Your presence and see Your hand at work in very real and tangible ways. As they are put in positions of ministering words of comfort to the dying, help them also give Your peace and invitation to eternal salvation. Empower these Chaplains to make a difference in the lives of soldiers and their families all around the world.

Help them minister to the sick and the well, the fit and the wounded.

Be gracious to them as they uproot themselves and their families to move anywhere You send them. Help them and their families adjust quickly to new bases, new schools, new friends, new homes, new foods, perhaps even new environments or languages. Draw their spouses and children to You at a young age, and help them understand the important role their loved one plays in the lives and eternities of those they serve.

Uphold the families of Chaplains. Even though so much around them changes so often, protect them. Surround them with angels to meet their needs. Help them make friends easily and acclimate to whatever is new, quickly. And cause them to see You have already gone before them wherever they are sent. Establish Your presence in their lives so strongly that they know, beyond a shadow of doubt, that they can rely on You, no matter the need. Amen.

# APPENDIX D

# Bonus Week of Prayers for Spiritual Power and Protection

Sometimes you feel the enemy is hitting you hard.
Well here at 40 Day Prayer Guides we humbly suggest
that in the name and power of the Lord Jesus Christ
you go right ahead and hit back.

**1—*Hezekiah's prayer***
***2 Kings 19:15-17, 19, 32-34***

2 Kings 19:15

*Lord, God of Israel, enthroned between the cherubim,*

*Lord, God of Israel, enthroned between the cherubim, You alone are God over all the kingdoms of the earth. You have made heaven and earth. Give ear, Lord, and hear; open Your eyes Lord, and see, listen to the words* **of the world and the evil one**, *sent to ridicule the living God.*

*It is true, Oh Lord, that* the evil one *has attacked and laid waste* **to many pastors and many churches, winning victories over their lives and the reputations of their congregations.** *Now, Lord, our God, deliver* Pastor \_\_\_\_, their family, and our church *from the hand of the enemy*

—from any plot or plan to derail the purpose and plan You have for their life, their family, or our church and its reputation in our community

—from any lies or deception the world or the evil one would use to oppress them

—from any harm the enemy would seek to do in their life, whether physical, mental, emotional, psychological, intellectual, social, financial, political or spiritual

*so that all the kingdoms of the earth may know that You, alone, Lord, are God.*

Father, Pastor \_\_\_\_ may not have to do battle on horseback with spears, like Hezekiah, but their enemies are real. Powers and forces come against their marriage, children, health, emotions, finances, life circumstances; all trying to defeat them and cause them to question or lose their faith.

Your response to Hezekiah was positive and powerful. I ask on behalf of my pastor, for the same victory you gave him:

The enemy *will not enter* Pastor _____'s life or the lives of their loved ones or launch an attack against them. The enemy *will not come before them with shield or build a siege ramp against* them to gain a foothold in their lives or cause devastation within their family. *By the way that the enemy came* to oppress them, *he will return* and will not enter. *You will defend* Pastor _____ *and save* them and their family, *for Your own sake*.

You have the power, the authority and the desire to act for Pastor _____. Thank You that You can do immeasurably more than I can ask, or even imagine, in their life, and in the lives of their loved ones - so that You will get all the glory! Amen

### 2—Colossians 1 Prayer
### Colossians 1:3-4, 9-12

Colossians 1:3, *We always thank God, the Father of our Lord Jesus Christ, when we pray for you...*

Heavenly Father, *I thank You* and praise You for Pastor _____. *Thank You for their faith in You and the love they have for all Your people* and for our church.

Father, *fill* Pastor _____ *with the knowledge of Your will* for their personal life and for our church. Do not let them be swayed by pressure from anyone else who might think to manipulate or control them. But give them Your insight and perspective, Your good and perfect will for them personally:

- in relation to You, their Father: how You would have them use the gifts and talents You have given them, what their worship looks like, and how they study to understand Your Word and apply it to their own life.
- in the roles they play: child, sibling, spouse, parent, friend. Show pastor _____ how to respond in every relationship You have given them.
- what Your will looks like in their service through the ministry You have given them in our church as leader, counselor, and shepherd.

Father, do this *through all the wisdom and understanding that the Spirit gives*.
- Not the wisdom of the world,
- or the logic of the mind,
- or the sense of the flesh.

These sources of "wisdom" do not serve Your purpose, but only confuse and distract. The fruit from these sources is not the Fruit of the Spirit which we seek: love, joy, peace, patience, goodness, kindness, gentleness, faithfulness and self-control.

Lead Pastor _____ in this way *so they may live a life worthy of You, pleasing You in every way: bearing fruit in every good work, and growing in the knowledge You give.*

And Father, *strengthen Pastor _____ with all power according to Your glorious might* in whatever ways are needed for the circumstances they are experiencing:
- physically when they need healing, or a bolstering of their immune system to ward off known or unknown illness, or when they need increased strength or stamina to do the work You have placed before them, or to be able to enjoy recreational opportunities, or when they just need energy to last through the day;
- mentally when they need to focus, clear their mind of distracting thoughts, or need the diligence to take every thought captive to You, or to be alert to dangers around them;
- emotionally to deal with all the things that Pastor _____ sees and hears and experiences that seem overwhelming in scope, relief from discouragement, sadness, fear, anger, guilt, at all the unfairness and oppression around them, anxiousness at circumstances beyond their control whether near or far;
- spiritually - to have Pastor _____'s faith bolstered by the remembrance that no matter what—You are in control—that even if the fig tree does not blossom, no grapes appear on the vine, the olive crop fails and the fields produce no crops—they can still rejoice in YOU! Give them spiritual strength to recognize and combat the enemy, as they are dressed in your spiritual armor.

Father, *strengthen my Pastor _____ with all this power according to Your glorious might*. Not mere human power, but Your divine power acting in them, *so they may have great endurance and patience. And be able to joyfully give thanks to You, who has qualified them to share in Your inheritance, with Your holy people in the Kingdom of Light.* Amen

### 3—The Soldier's Psalm
### Psalm 91:1-16

Psalm 91:1, Whoever dwells in the shelter of the Most High will rest in the shadow of the Almighty.

Heavenly Father, Pastor _____ *dwells in Your shelter, let them rest in Your shadow*, the shadow of the Almighty. Pastor _____ will say of You, *"He is my refuge and my fortress, my God, in whom I trust,"* professing their faith in You.

*Surely* Father, *You will save them from the fowler's snare and from the deadly pestilence.* There are those who would set a trap for my pastor. Let Pastor _____

see a trap for what it is. Help them turn away from the lure on the hook that would ensnare them. There is enticement all around, and disease, but You, Father, can protect them. Strengthen their immune system so they won't get sick. Protect and heal them from illnesses, deadly diseases, and even epidemics.

Father, *cover* my Pastor _____ *with Your feathers, and under Your wings* they *will find refuge. Spread Your wings over* them like a mother hen gathers her chicks. Protect them from danger, accident, illness, trauma, and violence. Protect their relationships, home, finances, transportation, job. Protect their emotions and spirit from any attack of the evil one, from any ungodly influences, and from the pressures of the world. And even from their own flesh when their desires go against the good that You have in store for them.

Father, *Your faithfulness will be their shield* and a wall behind which they can find safety. Be their courage both day and night, not living or walking in fear of what attacks may come or what disaster might lie in wait. Watch over their comings and goings day and night.

Thank You that You never sleep, but keep watch all the time. Although *the enemy may fall at their side, ten thousand at your right hand, destruction will not come near* Pastor _____. They *will only observe with their eyes and see the punishment of the wicked.*

Let Pastor _____ say, "The LORD is my refuge," and make You, the Most High, their dwelling, *so that no harm overtakes* them, *no disaster comes near* their home or their family. But *command Your angels concerning* Pastor _____ and *guard* them *in all* their *ways*: as a marriage partner, a parent, a sibling, a friend, neighbor, and as a leader in our church and community. Send Your *angels to lift* Pastor _____ *up in their hands, so that* Pastor _____ *will not strike their foot against a stone* and trip or fall, physically, morally or spiritually.

Give my pastor victory over dangerous enemies: physical, political, and spiritual. Help them defeat all those who set themselves against You and against my Pastor and our church. Both those who walk this physical earth, and those who dwell in spiritual realms.

*"Because* this pastor *loves me,"* says the LORD, *"I will rescue them; I will protect* them, *for* they *acknowledge my name."* Father, remind Pastor _____ to *call on You in trouble* or they have any concern or need for themselves, their family, or our church. You promise to answer those prayers and be with them in any trouble. *Deliver them* from the enemy *and honor them.*

*Satisfy* Pastor _____ *with long life* as they delight in their salvation. Amen

## 4—A Psalm of David
### Psalm 35:1-10, 17-28

Psalm 35:1, *Contend Lord, with those who contend with me...*

Contend, Lord, with those who contend with Pastor _____; fight against those who fight against them.
Take up shield and armor; arise and come to their aid. Brandish spear and javelin against those who pursue Pastor _____.

Say to Pastor _____, "I am your salvation."
May those who seek my pastor's life be disgraced and put to shame; may those who plot Pastor _____'s ruin be turned back in dismay.

May they be like chaff before the wind, with the angel of the Lord driving them away; may their path be dark and slippery, with the angel of the Lord pursuing them.

Since they hid their net for Pastor _____ without cause and without cause dug a pit for them, may ruin overtake [those who set the traps] by surprise—may the net they hid entangle them, may they fall into the pit, to their ruin.

Then my soul will rejoice in the Lord and delight in His salvation.
My whole being will exclaim, "Who is like you, Lord?

How long, Lord, will you look on? Rescue Pastor _____ from the ravages, their precious life from these lions.

I will give you thanks in the great assembly; among the throngs I will praise you.

Do not let those gloat over my pastor who are their enemies without cause; do not let those who hate Pastor _____ without reason maliciously wink the eye.

They do not speak peaceably, but devise false accusations against those who live quietly in the land. They sneer at Pastor _____ and say, "Aha! Aha! With our own eyes we have seen it."

Lord, you have seen this; do not be silent. Do not be far from my pastor Lord. Awake, and rise to Pastor _____'s defense! Contend for them, my God and Lord. Vindicate Pastor _____ in your righteousness, Lord my God; do not let them gloat over my pastor. Do not let them think, "Aha, just what we wanted!" or say, "We have swallowed them up."

May all who gloat over Pastor _____'s distress be put to shame and confusion; may all who exalt themselves over them be clothed with shame and disgrace.

May those who delight in Pastor _____'s vindication shout for joy and gladness; may they always say, "The Lord be exalted, who delights in the well-being of his servant."

My tongue will proclaim your righteousness, Your praises all day long. **Amen**

**5—A song David sang to the Lord**
**Psalm 7:1, 6-13, 17**

Psalm 7:1, *Lord my God, I take refuge in you…*

Heavenly Father, Pastor \_\_\_\_ *takes refuge in you; save and deliver them from all who pursue them.* There are so many who delight in seeing a pastor fail. By choosing to serve You with their life, my pastor has accepted a target on their back from the evil one.

The evil one seeks to keep my pastor fearful, discouraged, frustrated, and make their faith in You waver. The devil desires Pastor \_\_\_\_'s financial ruin, the destruction of their marriage, the smearing of their reputation, and personal moral failure.

The enemy is always crouching at my pastor's door, waiting to devour them. The flesh, the world, and the evil one are all influences that war against Your wisdom Father, Your plan and Your purpose for Pastor \_\_\_\_'s life.

So I ask, *"Arise, Lord, in Your anger; rise up against the rage of* Pastor \_\_\_\_*'s enemies. Awake my God; and decree justice. O righteous God, who searches minds and hearts of people, and judges* them. *Vindicate* my pastor *O Most High… bring to an end the violence of the wicked and make the righteous secure.*

Pastor \_\_\_\_*'s shield is God Most High, who saves the upright in heart…you will not relent* or back down from the fight, *but will sharpen your sword; and will bend and string your bow. You have prepared deadly weapons; and have made ready Your flaming arrows."*

Defend Pastor \_\_\_\_ against all that seeks to destroy them, their godly relationships, their adoration and worship of You, their ministry in Your name, and their freedom to read and study Your Word.

And Pastor \_\_\_\_ *will give thanks to You because of Your righteousness and will sing praise to your name: The Lord Most High.* Amen

### 6—Real-time Protection as Pastors preach

Jeremiah 1:7, *But the L*ORD *said to me, "...*
You must go to everyone I send you to and say whatever I command you. *Do not be afraid of them, for I am with you and will rescue you," declares the L*ORD.

Heavenly Father, I believe that as Pastor \_\_\_\_ preaches Your Word with transparency and power, that many people will be freed - from fear, from anxiety, from darkness, from so many things the evil one uses to keep people trapped in their unbelief.

As Pastor \_\_\_\_ preaches give them power and clarity of thought and speech to preach Your words clearly and boldly. Stir their passion! Fill them with the power to speak Your name with authority over the enemy so that nothing would hurt them (Luke 10:19). And open the ears of every listener to be able to hear and understand the Holy Spirit speaking through these messages. Prepare the listeners' hearts to hear the Good News and receive salvation.

Go before my pastor into every place they will speak Your Word. Allow Your presence to be felt in the gathering places and send away any and every presence that is not of You. Foil the plans and the strategies of the evil one and protect everyone in attendance. We ally ourselves in prayer with the power of the blood and the name of our Lord Jesus Christ, and in this power demand that the devil be sent away from all planned and unplanned gatherings and presentations of the Gospel or Christian testimony.

We pray against any other rulers: acknowledging that You are the one and only King. All glory and honor are due You and not to any other ruler on earth or above or beneath the earth.

To those who have been given authority by the evil one, we acknowledge that only You have the authority over all of Creation and over every living being You have created. And because we are Your sons and daughters, You are our only true authority.

Against the powers of this dark world, we bring Your Light. You *are* Light and You dispel the darkness, stripping away any power the evil one might have given those who serve him. And we bring the power of the Name of the Lord Jesus Christ and His precious blood against the spiritual forces in the heavenly realms.

Thank You for how You have worked in Pastor \_\_\_\_ and their family to bring them to this place. Thank You for giving Pastor \_\_\_\_ the messages they preach. Holy Spirit, fall on us as we listen. Let us hear with understanding how to apply the truth to our lives. Revive us! Amen

### 7—When Saul sent men to watch David's house in order to kill him
### Psalm 59:1-5, 9-10, 12-13, 16-17

Psalm 59:1, *Deliver me from my enemies, O God...*
*Deliver* Pastor _____ *from* their *enemies, O God;*
be their *fortress against those who are attacking them.*
*Deliver* Pastor _____ *from evildoers*
and save my pastor *from those who are after* their *blood.*
*See how* the enemies *lie in wait for* them!
*Fierce men conspire against* my pastor
*for no offense or sin of* theirs, L ORD.
They *have done no wrong, yet* enemies *are ready to attack* my pastor.
*Arise to help* Pastor _____*; look on* their *plight!*
*You,* L ORD *God Almighty, you who are the God of Israel,*
*rouse yourself to punish all the* enemy; *show no mercy to wicked traitors.*

*You are* Pastor _____*'s strength,* they *watch for you; you, God, are* their *fortress,* my pastor's *God on whom* they *can rely.*

*God will go before* my pastor *and will let* my pastor *gloat over those who slander* them. *For the sins of their mouths, for the words of their lips, let them be caught in their pride. For the curses and lies they utter, consume them in your wrath, consume them till they are no more. Then it will be known to the ends of the earth that God rules over Jacob.*

Pastor _____ *will sing of your strength, in the morning* they *will sing of your love; for you are* my pastor's *fortress,* their *refuge in times of trouble.*

*You are* Pastor _____*'s strength,* they *sing praise to you; you, God, are* their *fortress,* their *God on whom* they *can rely.* Amen

# APPENDIX E

## How You Tune in to God's Voice

I believe God is speaking to us, or sending out His signal, all the time, through His Word, His Son, His Creation, and our circumstances, among other ways. His is a constant, uninterruptible, full-strength signal. But we need to tune in to hear it.

God has given us, built into us, a receiver to hear Him. It's our spirit. We are all made up of body, mind and spirit. As a believer, we also have the Holy Spirit within us who helps us hear Him even better. And the Holy Spirit helps us understand what we hear.

His is a perfect "wireless" connection that is never out of service, out of range, broken, interrupted by weather conditions, satellite position, or earthly circumstances. But here are three reasons we may not be "tuned in."

1 We don't know God's frequencies?

> Prayer—Scripture—Nature—Circumstances—
> Dreams—Pain—Sermons—Bible Study—
> People—Podcasts—Christian books—Revelations

Ask yourself—Are you tuning in to and exposing yourself to the sources God is broadcasting on?

> Make time for those opportunities regularly in your day, your week. Ask God to speak to you in ways you will notice and understand. You might try a "Tune In Exercise" in the next section of the Appendix.

2 Like your physical ears, we can't hear clearly if the noise level around us is drowning out what God is saying. And we have inner voices we often focus on that keep us from hearing what God has to say.

Ask yourself—Are you paying more attention to what you hear in the world and within yourself?

> Invite the Holy Spirit to silence all ungodly sources and distractions. Ask that confusion, preconceived ideas, biases, and

misconceptions be sent away. And ask the Holy Spirit to reveal truth, clarify meaning, and show application to your life.

3  You have an ear infection. Spiritually, sin can block our ability to communicate effectively with God.

Ask yourself—Have you cleaned out your spiritual ears lately?

Be willing to confess your sin to God and turn from it. He will forgive you and that will re-establish your communication.

For more information, see Confession and Repentance in Appendix A.

# APPENDIX F

# Tune in Exercise for Hearing God

God speaks in so many different ways, I can't list them all. He is so creative and you are unique. Here are 4 exercises you can try that have worked for others.

Begin by asking God to speak to you in a way that you will recognize and understand. He WILL answer your prayer. Although it can happen, you may not hear an audible, physical voice.

1—Set aside a time to get alone and just be still. Arrange for no interruptions. Turn off your cell phone or anything else that might distract you. For some people it helps to be outdoors without the distractions of the house or apartment. For others, a quiet room works.

Start a conversation with God. You can speak out loud, or with your inner voice, He can hear you. Begin by thanking God - for who He is, for something He's done in your life or in the world. Or begin with a question you have, or share with Him something that's weighing on your heart or concerning you.

Then quiet yourself and listen. Eyes open are ok unless that distracts you. Eyes closed works too. Ask the Holy Spirit to help you sense what God is saying. He may speak to you in words of comfort, or love, instruction or change your perspective. He may place a picture or vision in your mind. He may sing you a song or direct you to scripture.

Write down what you hear. Then check it against scripture in the Hearing God Worksheet in the Appendix.

2—Plan uninterrupted time without others nearby to observe what is around you.

If you can go outside, are there birds, trees, flowers, clouds, mountains, water, some piece of God's creation that might have a message for you? Do you see something that shows you something about yourself, or about God? Do you see something that reflects some inner truth?

If inside, look out a window, or at art, or the colors or items around you and check any memories or feelings they evoke. Do you need a fresh look at an area of your life? Do you need help dealing with emotions that may have surfaced?

3—Get alone in a comfortable place where you can read or listen. Open your Bible or listen to scripture being read aloud. If you've been reading regularly, start where you left off. If not you might consider looking at the One Year Bible website and choose the scripture selection for that day. God may direct you to a place to begin. If this is new to you, start with the book of John. Or Joshua. Or 1 John.

Start reading and read until you hear something that resonates with something you are going through. It may be a message of instruction, or encouragement, or a revelation about yourself or God. A verse may stand out with a new significance or a better understanding than it has had before. Or it may shine a light that gives you a new perspective.

Ask what this means. And what it means to you. Is there something you need to change—to do, or stop doing with this new understanding? Is there a warning you need to heed? An example for you to follow? Is God showing you something about Himself? About yourself in these verses?

4—Freestyle—Talk to God Wherever you are, whenever—day or night, whatever the circumstances. You can say anything to Him. Whisper your fears, yell your frustrations, rage against your circumstances. He can take it all. Pour out your heart about what you are facing. Ask for His perspective. Or for clarification on an issue.

Are you experiencing blessing? Confusion? Pain? What in your circumstances is speaking the loudest? Ask God to show you where He is in that circumstance and ask Him for wisdom to cope with it. What you can learn from it. How can you share the blessing? What can you learn from your pain? Who can you connect with because of your blessing, confusion or pain?

Then pause to hear His answer. Do you need a change of attitude? A course correction? Do you hear a word of encouragement? Direction? Or feel a sense of comfort? Can you comfort, direct or encourage someone else with what you hear?

# APPENDIX G

# Hearing from God

Proverbs 8:32-5 *"Now then, my children, listen to me;*
*blessed are those who keep my ways.*
*Listen to my instruction and be wise;*
*do not disregard it.*
*Blessed are those who listen to me,*
*watching daily at my doors,*
*waiting at my doorway.*
*For those who find me find life*
*and receive favor from the Lord.*

**B**ut how do I know if what I hear is from God or some other voice?? When you believe you've heard from God You, write it down and put it to the test.

Ask these three questions to see if you heard it from God or some other source:

### 1—Does what I hear agree with the Bible?

**The answer must be "yes."** God will never tell you anything that contradicts what He has already said in His Word. So, spend time in and be familiar with the Bible.

If you need help, a Christian friend or pastor can help you find scripture dealing with your topic. If there is nothing, or you are unsure, ask God to reveal the truth to you.

One role of the Holy Spirit who dwells in every believer is to teach us, guiding us in truth. In John 14:26, Jesus tells us the Holy Spirit will teach us all things. And in John 16:13 tells us the Holy Spirit will guide us into all truth.

### 2—Will the result, or the fruit of the act be the fruit of the Spirit?

**This answer should also be "yes."** The result of what you hear should lead to and produce the fruit of the Spirit in your life and those around you.

Galatians 5:19-23 outlines the fruit of the Spirit as: love, joy, peace, patience, kindness, goodness, faithfulness, gentleness, and self-control.

Verses 19-21 tell us the acts of the flesh are immorality, impurity, debauchery, idolatry, witchcraft, hatred, discord, jealousy, rage, selfish ambition, dissension, envy, and the like.

So if you act on what you think God is telling you, what will happen? Look at the expected result, or the "fruit," to see where it leads.

### 3 - Will it benefit my relationship with God?

Again, **this answer should be "yes."** Everything you do will benefit or weaken your relationship with God.

Micah 6:8 *And what does the Lord require of you? To act justly and to love mercy and to* walk humbly with *your God.*

Most of the time, the Holy Spirit will tell you if what you are doing is pulling you away from God. You will probably be able to sense that you are either drawing closer to God or pulling away if you were to follow through on what you think you hear Him telling you.

It might help to ask another Christian friend, pastor or counselor. Or even pose the question: What Would Jesus do?

**If you hit a "no" stop right there!** What you heard is **NOT from God**. If it
**does NOT agree with the Bible**, or
**does NOT produce the Fruit of the Spirit**, or
**does NOT benefit your relationship with God**,
then it is NOT from God.

**So what do you do** ?

If you got a NO -

Pray for strength to say "no" to that and keep seeking God's wisdom.

James 1:5 says *"If any of you lacks wisdom, you should ask God, who gives generously to all without finding fault, and it will be given to you."* So ask again for God's input.

If you got 3 YES -

Pray for the strength and courage to follow through on what God has shown you.

Paul encourages us that we can do all things through Christ who strengthens us. Philippians 4:13

If confusion still exists, go back and ask God for clarity. And be patient. The answer may be unclear because the timing isn't right. Be willing to wait on God's timing.

Psalm 27:14 *Wait* for *the Lord; be strong and take heart and wait* for *the Lord.*

# APPENDIX H

## Hearing from God Worksheet

Is what I'm hearing from God?

**James 1:5** *If any of you lacks wisdom, you should ask God, who gives generously to all without finding fault, and it will be given to you.*

If you hit a "No" stop there. Is it NOT from God.

| |
|---|
| What is my concern or question |
| What am I hearing? |
| What does the Bible say about my concern and what I am hearing? |
| Does what I am hearing agree with the Bible? ❏Y ❏N |
| If I act on what I've heard, what will it produce in my life and others? |
| Is that a Fruit of the Spirit? ❏Y ❏N |
| If I act on what I've heard, will it benefit my relationship with God? ❏Y ❏N |

# APPENDIX I
## List of Images, by Day

**Cover**—Cumulonimbus cloud, i.e. Thunderhead in Colorado's Front Range
**Intro**—Montezuma's Tower climb, Garden of the Gods, Colorado Springs, Colorado
**Foreword**—Dusk, driving through Everglades NP
**Another Battle lyrics**—Wintertime blossoms, Oahu, Hawaii
**Day 1**—Virgin River Narrows, Zion NP
**Day 2**—Beach outside Naval Air Station (NAS) Pensacola, FL, home of the Blue Angels
**Day 3**—American Alligator, Big Cypress National Preserve, Florida
**Day 4**—Class V 'Sunshine Falls' rapid, Royal Gorge of the Arkansas River, Canon City, Colorado
**Day 5**—Desert bighorn sheep, with this year's kiddos, near Montrose, Colorado
**Day 6**—Scouting a rapid along Deso/Grey Canyon on the Green River in Utah
**Day 7**—Rim Trail, Royal Gorge, Canon City, Colorado
**Day 8**—Red Rock Canyon Open Space, Colorado Springs, Colorado
**Day 9**—Autumn aspen trees, outside Cimarron, Colorado
**Day 10**—Nankoweep, Grand Canyon NP
**Day 11**—'Driving' near Savannah, GA
**Day 12**—'Bridge' move on a slot canyon approach in Zion NP
**Day 13**—'Noble Hammock' paddle trail, Everglades NP
**Day 14**—Horsing around in whitewater with friends
**Day 15**—South Kaibab Trail, Grand Canyon NP
**Day 16**—Pack train, crossing the South Fork, Flathead River, Montana wilderness
**Day 17**—Mile 248, running the Colorado River through Grand Canyon NP
**Day 18**—Local parks, Savannah, GA
**Day 19**—'Corner Pocket' rapid, Arkansas River
**Day 20**—Scouting 'Upset' rapid, Colorado River through Grand Canyon NP
**Day 21**—Via Ferrata in Ouray, Colorado
**Day 22**—Banyan trees near Pt Charlotte, Florida
**Day 23**—Red Rock Canyon Open Space, Colorado Springs, Colorado
**Day 24**—Pinned boat, Arkansas River
**Day 25**—Redwall Cavern, Grand Canyon NP
**Day 26**—Crack climbing in Indian Creek, Utah ('Optimator Wall' for you serious climbers)
**Day 27**—Boardwalk Trail, Big Cypress National Preserve, Florida

**Day 28**—Lost Creek Wilderness area, Colorado
**Day 29**—Waterfall along the 3-day Routeburn Track, South Island, New Zealand
**Day 30**—Shoreline near Boca Grande, Florida
**Day 31**—Side hike, Colorado River through Grand Canyon NP
**Day 32**—'Travertine Falls' side hike , Mile 229 along Colorado River through Grand Canyon NP
**Day 33**—Class III 'Spikebuck Falls' rapid, Bighorn Sheep Canyon section of the Arkansas River, Canon City, Colorado
**Day 34**—Autumn trees by fountain, Centennial Park, Canon City, Colorado
**Day 35**—Small church in the farmland surrounding LeClaire, Iowa
**Day 36**—Setting sun, Garden of the Gods, Colorado Springs, Colorado
**Day 37**—'Pancake Rocks' hike, Pike National Forest
**Day 38**—Via Ferrata in Ouray, Colorado
**Day 39**—Ice Climbing at North Cheyenne Canyon, Colorado Springs, Colorado
**Day 40**—Church steeple during the 2012 Waldo Canyon wildfire near Colorado Springs, Colorado
**After 40**—Colorado mountains near Breckenridge, Colorado
**Thank You After 40 Days**—Shoreline at Blue Mesa Reservoir near Gunnison, Colorado
**Appendices**—Colorado Front Range electrical storm, baby!

**Interlude and Reflection** images (in no order)—
1. Herman Gulch hike, near Silverthorne, Colorado
2. Oat grass along shore, Bradenton, Florida
3. 'Silver Grotto' hike, Colorado River through Grand Canyon NP
4. Nighttime, Everglades NP
5. Riverbank, Arkansas River, Colorado
6. Red grass meadow outside Queenstown, New Zealand

# About the Authors

### Eric Sprinkle

A former Whitewater Guide and Swift-water Rescue Instructor for the U.S. military, Eric travels the country speaking about the benefits of risk, managing fear, and how to make life more exciting by "living a slightly more dangerous lifestyle." He calls the multi-sport playground of Colorado Springs home and was 'that kid' who could never, ever sit still in church. Sorry about that pastors…

If any of the book's images capture or inspire you? That's Jesus' fault for giving him traits like Risk-Taking, Daring, and being Adventurous.

Find more about him at AdventureExperience. net, including Speaker info, free book images, and an action-packed YouTube channel full of waterfalls, cliff faces, and whitewater silliness.

### Laura Shaffer

An Army Brat moving almost every year till college, Laura was delighted to discover that wherever she went, God was always there ahead of her. Even though the houses, schools and friends changed, there was always church or Military Chapel where she learned that God was always with her. And she felt it.

She continues to sense God's presence working in the yard, taking walks in beautiful, colorful Colorado and through prayer.

It's her desire to encourage you to lean into God and learn from Him, and to empower your prayer life and deepen your relationship with God.

Check out Laura's blog at www.DailyBiblePrayer.wordpress.com for scripture-based examples of her prayers anytime.

# APPENDIX J
## Additional Resources

*For busy pastors who spend enough time on building maintenance, youth activities, and putting together a sermon each week, where do you find the time to work with those folks who keep asking about community outreach programs?*

*Maybe have a look at a book from Toni, a friend of ours, and see if that might bring a solution.*

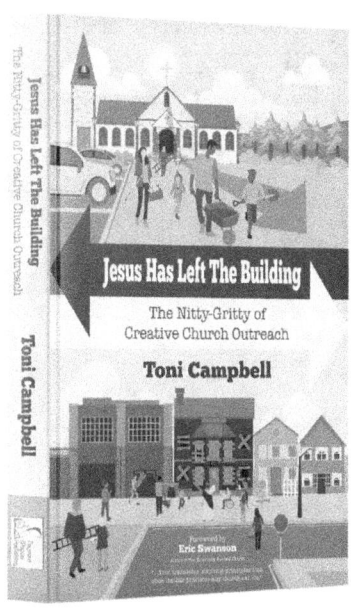

# Jesus Has Left The Building

## The Nitty Gritty of Creative Church Outreach

Community outreach is important, but when you already wear a dozen hats, where do you find the time? What if you could put a book with step-by-step instructions for a dozen different ideas into the hands of that group of movers and shakers in your church and watch things take off? My award-winning book, *Jesus Has Left the Building: The Nitty Gritty of Creative Church Outreach* can do just that. It's filled with practical ideas, the details to execute them, resources to finance them, and stories to warm your heart.

| | |
|---|---|
| ISBN: | 978-1736008003 |
| Publisher: | Pageant Wagon Publishing |
| Format: | Paperback |
| Price: | $14.99 |
| Publication date: | August 31, 2021 |

Available through:

"If you'll spend time with these 12 great outreach ideas from Toni Campbell, you won't be the same...nor will your church...nor will your community...highly readable, engaging, practical, doable, and quite often fun!"

**Warren Bird, Ph.D.,**
Author/co-author of 33 books for church leaders

"What Toni does is translate inspiring principles into shoe leather practices that any church could do and every church should do - if they want to follow Jesus into the community and be an agency in its transformation...all you need to start making a Kingdom ruckus in your community."

**Eric Swanson**
*The Externally Focused Church*

## About the author

Toni Campbell pioneered a high impact community outreach ministry and has been specializing in creative, interactive projects for over a decade. Her experience organizing a small army of over 100 volunteers in these innovative projects that extend beyond church walls is the basis of this book. In 2012, Toni was awarded Mercer County's (NJ) Woman of Achievement Award for her accomplishments and the immense impact they made on the community.

# Additional Thoughts on Praying for Your Pastor

# LOVE LAURA'S PRAYERS?

Looking for more from your new prayer partner Laura?

You've got it!

Have a look here for daily prayers, inspiring blogs, and more!

Check out her prayer blog—
www.dailyBibleprayer.wordpress.com
For her devotion blog—
www.hearmorefromGod.wordpress.com

LISTEN UP!
Lean in & Learn from the Lord™

# Additional Thoughts on Praying for Your Pastor

## Need an Adventure Speaker for your next event or group meet-up?

Need someone to talk about
- Risk and Challenge
- Making your life more Exciting
- Dealing better with Fear

Eric would love to hang out with your group!

He's ready to unpack the question of whether our Lord God calls us to adventure, and even share some fun stories about prayer books too! All with heart pounding stories and gorgeous photos!

Check out AdventureExperience.net today and let's connect for an inspiring, challenging time together!

# Additional Thoughts on Praying for Your Pastor

# More from Adventure Experience Press

**Adventure Devos:** The first devotional written exclusively for men with a heart for Risk and Danger

**Adventure Devos: Women's Edition:** An exciting devotional written exclusively for women with a Heart for Risk and Adventure

**Adventure Devos: Youth Edition:** Summer Camp never has to end when your devotional takes you adventuring all year long!

"Adventure Devos will challenge any man to be a better father or husband in no time, no doubt about it. Just read a few of the book's "Dares" and see for yourself how easily this devotional will get anyone into applying God's Word.
Megan "Katniss" Autrey, Colorado Certified Whitewater Guide Instructor, Wife and Mother

# Additional Thoughts on Praying for Your Pastor

# 40DayPrayerGuides.com

Looking for another 40-Day Prayer Journey? Want to share and inspire others with stories from your last one? Welcome to the 40 Day Prayer Guide Series!

## Be the first to download and check samples of the latest Guides, always weeks before they're listed for sale!

- Download free samples to share with friends
- Have a look at what's coming next in the 40-Day Prayer Guides series
- Share thoughts, ideas, and praises from your own 40-day journeys!

*"This is a powerful book and is very much needed."*
*"I know several in my church right now who I plan to give copies to—real prayer warriors who would love this tool!"*
(Early Reader Feedback)

*Come have a look, sign up for the Newsletter and be more inspired in your prayer life today!*

# Additional Thoughts on Praying for Your Pastor

# Also available in the 40 Day Prayer Guide Series
### 40DayPrayerGuides.com

Ready-made prayers for someone's **Salvation, Blessings** for a friend, or asking for more **Godly Character**

## THE PRAYERS ARE FOR THEM, THE JOURNEY IS FOR YOU

### COMING SOON!
**Recovering from a Mistake** editions and much more! Grab one today!

# Additional Thoughts on Praying for Your Pastor